'BAMA FOOTBALL MYTHS

Also by Jacob M. Carter

Before History Dies
The RipTide
The Table of Truth

My Hope is Build on Nothing Less
Edward Mote
Public Domain

'Bama Football Myths
Copyright © 2019
Jacob M. Carter

ISBN: 978-1-948679-91-6

All rights reserved. No part of this book may be reproduced, stored in a retrieval system, or transmitted in any form or by any means—electronic, mechanical, photocopy, recording or otherwise—without the prior written permission of the publisher. The only exception is brief quotations for review purposes.

Published by WordCrafts Press
Cody, Wyoming 82414
www.wordcrafts.net

'BAMA FOOTBALL MYTHS

Jacob M. Carter

WordCrafts

Dedication

This book is dedicated to Alabama fans.
You are crazy, but I am too.

Contents

Foreword 1
Introduction 5
Alabama was Lucky Colt McCoy was Injured 10
Alabama Didn't Deserve to Play in the 2011-2012 National Championship 14
Alabama Always Plays a Weak Schedule 18
Alabama Players Bust in the NFL 22
Auburn is on Alabama's Level 25
Nick Saban is a Terrible Person 28
Alabama hasn't had a Legit Quarterback Since Tua Tagovailoa 32
The Officials Cheat for Alabama 35
Alabama Pays Its Players 39
Alabama Fans are the Worst 42
Alabama didn't Deserve to be in the 2017 Playoff 45
Alabama Claims too many Championships 49
Nick Saban Pushes Assistants Away 52
Kirby Smart is the next Nick Saban 55
When Alabama Loses the Dynasty is Dead 57
Coach Saban Doesn't Discipline his Players 60
Nick Saban was a Terrible NFL Coach 65
Alabama is Boring to Watch 68
Closing 71
Quotes 76
Write Me Your Memories 81
A Letter to my Fellow Alabama Fans 84
An Open Letter from Stan J. Griffin 86
My Greatest Experiences as an Alabama Fan 89
Thoughts on the Afterlife 95
Author's Note 97
Acknowledgments & References 99
About the Author 101

Foreword

If you've ever met my friend Jacob Carter, then you are also probably keenly aware of his tremendous passion for all things related to University of Alabama football, and the rich tradition that defines the most illustrious college football program in the history of the sport.

I can certainly relate, being born and raised in Tuscaloosa, graduating from UA in 1993, and covering Crimson Tide football for various publications going back to the Gene Stallings era. Being a true and passionate Alabama football supporter means carrying yourself with a bit of extra confidence and swagger, even to the point of being a bit obnoxious and arrogant at times.

This has been the case for those who "bleed Crimson" during the past 12 years of the Nick Saban era at the Capstone, one of the true generational dynasties in the long history of the sport we love so passionately. This allegiance to the UA gridiron legacy, however, also means dealing with the multitude of Alabama haters out there.

There are many delusional and desperate types who will say just about anything to discredit the accomplishments of the iconic Crimson Tide program, even if it means putting their obvious vitriol and bitterness regarding Tide football on full display, as well as their limited knowledge about college football in general at times. Whether it be on social media, on internet discussion forums, or even at the local sports bar, being an Alabama football fan means dealing with people who want to mock or debate everything about your program. These debates are far reaching. They could be about the amount of national titles the Crimson Tide program claims, Alabama's position in the hierarchy of the sport, or even about whether or not much of the success that Alabama has gained under Paul "Bear" Bryant and Saban among other Tide coaches is largely due to good luck, terrible schedules, and the media's love affair with the Crimson Tide program.

I know, those kinds of thoughts sound silly and petty for reasonable and intelligent people who fervently follow the sport and handle things with a deal of objectivity as well. But again, there are many who choose to forego all sense of logic and reason if they have a chance to devalue anything positive that the Crimson Tide has accomplished. Even if it means creating myths about Alabama football—such as the Crimson Tide always getting all the calls, that the bowl and playoff system has always favored Alabama because of its name, or the various conspiracies out there that state that Alabama always gets preferential treatment because it is in bed with the NCAA, the Southeastern Conference, or the various networks such as ESPN.

I think that one regarding the networks and their love affair with Alabama is especially funny as it would not take me long to compile a list of talking heads from various networks who have an obvious distaste for all things Crimson Tide, and they rarely try to hide it.

That is why my friend Jacob has produced this pocket book that you now hold, as he dispels many of those longstanding myths regarding the eternally-provocative Crimson Tide football program. You are now armed with a bit of ammunition as this book should allow you to confidently refute many of those misguided sentiments related to Alabama football and its long history of staggering success.

I guess one of my main pet peeve myths, or flat out lies, about the UA gridiron program is that much of the success that Alabama has attained under Saban is due to mediocre schedules. The last time I checked, even though Alabama has not had many great home games and home series during the Saban era other than the one against Penn State, the Crimson Tide has played a host of very attractive neutral site contests against the likes of Southern Cal, Louisville, Wisconsin, Florida State, Clemson, and Virginia Tech. It is not Alabama's fault if programs such as Louisville happened to be in a down cycle when these games occurred.

And most years, by the time the Crimson Tide has made it through the SEC title games, the playoff games and the national title tilts, besides the usually-tough SEC slate of games, the Alabama schedules do not take a back seat to many programs out there.

For example, the 2015 Alabama team that finished 14-1, captured the SEC title, and defeated Clemson to win the National Championship beat seven opponents that were ranked in the final Associated Press poll. The 2017 Alabama National Championship team only beat four teams that were ranked in the final AP poll that season but began the season with a win over a Florida State team ranked No. 3 at that point. After controversially making the four-team College Football Playoff field that same season, Alabama more than proved its merit by thumping No. 1 seed Clemson and then dispatching SEC champion Georgia with a dramatic comeback for the ages to gain its 17th national title.

I could go on and on about scheduling and a host of other Alabama football-related myths, but this is Jacob Carter's baby, and he does a great job in this book of setting the record straight regarding a lot of very false Crimson Tide folklore. That's why this work is worth a read for all Alabama football fans who truly and faithfully "bleed Crimson."

Stan J. Griffin

Stan J. Griffin is a freelance writer/photographer who is a native and resident of Tuscaloosa. He is a 1993 graduate of the University of Alabama and has covered Alabama football for a host of publications, including The Crimson White, Crimson Magazine, Druid City Living, Tidelines, Tide Sports Weekly, and newspapers such as The Andalusia Star News and St. Clair News-Aegis. He currently writes and does photography for publications such as Softball America and Tuscaloosa Magazine.

Introduction

Mythological origins are difficult to trace. Where do these stories come from? Who started them? How did they become accepted as a universal truth? These stories must have begun somewhere.

Well-told myths typically involve stories about supernatural feats. While they became exaggerated through time, I believe they start as a logical explanation about a particular event in the beginning. Yet, throughout history people have grown them into tall tales. They did this for several reasons. Some did it to create hope, or to enforce a code for living. Others did it for entertainment. No matter the reason, when one takes the time to study how humanity used to react to myths, a reoccurring theme appears: The world used to enjoy them.

However, in our post-modern word, things have changed. We no longer believe in anything. We want to debunk everything. Everything must be questioned, challenged, and shredded if it climbs too high into our negative worldview. Have you noticed that when someone achieves an incredible feat in our society, we tend to instantly work hard to discredit it through our own cynical outlook?

This battle of ruination is waged online, for the most part. No one is safe if they overachieve. Keyboard warriors and YouTube rangers stand on the web's watchtower, day-in and day-out, seeking which overachiever they can destroy next. In laymen's terms, some people want to discredit anything special, in any arena of life, for no other reason than the fact they are intoxicated on haterade.

This happens in many different realms of life. For example; a politician unexpectedly wins an election—*they cheated!* If a parent raised great children—*they got lucky.* A businesswoman makes a lot of money—*she must be corrupt.* It's that line of thinking that drove me to create this book.

Alabama football, despite all its achievements, is a victim to the greater psychological disposition in our society. The myths that have been created to discredit its dynasty are relentless and clever. They are clever, but they crumble once you begin to chip away at their inner core.

The only reason Alabama wins is because they cheat. I see that kind of statements tossed around comment sections, forums, and blogs as if they are facts. Year after year, Alabama sustains their program through recruiting great players, teaching them discipline, and applying tactical coaching. Year after year, trolls sustain their efforts to discredit that process through recruiting other trolls, teaching them laziness, and applying tactical fibbing. Instead of enjoying the reality of a modern day "mythical" accomplishment, these trolls seek to destroy it. Thus, the myths behind Alabama football have grown and grown into a disproportionate size. They flood the internet with innuendos that *Alabama can't really be this good. Surely, they are frauds.*

Yes, they can be that good, and no, they are not frauds! I'll tell you why.

In the following pages, you will read a systematic and

statistical debunking of the myths they have created. Those pesky things called "facts" will deliver a fatal blow upon those who have a strange craving to discredit my favorite college football program.

Yes, I am an Alabama fan. Yes, I am here to talk trash in this book. Yes, I do hope to arm other Alabama fans with the material they need to come against the false facts online, or wherever else they choose to promote them.

This pocket guide is for you—my fellow 'Bama fan. It's time to rise and defend the dynasty! Stop believing the myths the trolls have created and repeated. They might sound plausible, but they are easily shredded under the microscope of research. Numbers don't lie—haters do. This book is my way of contributing to the work of Nick Saban and company. It's a way to establish what's already true—Alabama is the greatest college football program of all time. This isn't just some biased opinion coming from my own fanhood. It is truth thoroughly backed up with evidence.

In the following pages you'll sift through different myths such as "Alabama cheats" and "Alabama gets lucky." As you read, you'll quickly develop a sense of how ridiculous some of these claims are. You'll also clearly see that Alabama has earned every accolade it has received. It wasn't because the referees got paid, nor was it an international conspiracy with Russia that got them into the playoffs. They didn't win championship after championship because they pay their players, or because key players on other teams got injured. The Crimson Tide won those championships because they are just that good.

And that's really the root reason why trolls seek to destroy the program. They just cannot seem to accept the fact that people can get together and achieve something admirable. But

Alabama football proves they can. With all the humor, jabbing, and fun this book brings the Alabama fanbase, I also want it to achieve another goal. I want to celebrate great accomplishments, wherever they happen. I want it to show great things can be accomplished.

Not everything good has to be a lie.
Not everyone strong takes steroids.
Not everyone smart cheats on their homework.
Not everything positive needs to be destroyed so someone can feel better about their own mediocrity.

Some things in life are just, well, incredible. Do we really want to live in a world where everything is always normal and bland? Do we want the trolls to destroy everything for their own amusement?

I hope not.

Alabama football has been a flagship program that's operated and succeeded through class and old school principles. The result of that philosophy has been proven on the gridiron, and ultimately in the trophy case. I'm tired of seeing people try to discredit it.

Why can't they just accept it and move on? They claim Alabama fans are arrogant and unreasonable, yet they are the ones who refuse to acknowledge what's blatantly obvious. The Crimson Tide has dominated for over a decade and will continue to do so. It's okay to accept that. As a matter of fact, for Auburn fans especially, it will be healthy for you. Think of it this way. You can stop trying to find reasons for why Alabama is good and start focusing on why your team isn't. Wow, that one even hurt me to write—not really.

So, fellow Alabama fan, I hope you enjoy this little book. I hope you use it as a tool to win the debates online. I hope it spreads far and wide. I hope the college football world knows they have, and still are, witnessing greatness.

The Golden State Warriors, the New England Patriots, the New York Yankees, Floyd Mayweather, the United States Olympic teams are great because... they're great. It's that simple. Each has been preyed upon by the *they must be frauds* trolls. Each rose above it, and consistently added to their gold medals, championship trophies, and record-setting performances. Let the trolls choke on that.

Myth #1

ALABAMA WAS LUCKY COLT McCOY WAS INJURED

Everything is bigger in Texas—including their excuses for losing to Alabama in the 2010 BCS National Championship game. As someone who personally lived in Texas, I'm here to testify why those excuses belong in the genre of fantasy. Bring up Alabama's Rose Bowl title win, and a Texas fan will immediately retort that if their star quarterback, Colt McCoy, had not got injured the Texas Longhorns would have easily won the game. They say Alabama got lucky.

While I will admit that his injury did hurt the Longhorns' chances, the thought that it was the lone deciding factor defies logic. The truth is Alabama decided to rely on a strong running game led by the duo of Trent Richardson and Heisman trophy winner Mark Ingram.

They also sat back in a basic defense and opted to force Texas to pass. This meant Texas had virtually no running game, and it hurt them in the long run as Alabama's offense out gunned Mack Brown's defense.

As former Alabama football defensive lineman, Lorenzo Washington explains, *"They weren't running the football on us. They didn't move the ball on us with their running game all night. On run plays, the only time they had the ball on a short field in the first half was on onside kicks."*

Washington went on to say, "*We weren't really rushing or pressuring. We were just playing our normal defense. Their defense was pretty good, but we outplayed them on defense, and our offense was putting up points, so I think it basically would have been the same result.*"

What Lorenzo was saying is that had Colt McCoy not gotten injured the result would have remained the same. Alabama would have won because the Texas Longhorn's defense could not stop Alabama's running game, nor could their own offense effectively run the ball against Nick Saban's defense.

When Texas fans say Alabama was *lucky* Colt McCoy was injured, I counter it wasn't luck at all. McCoy left the game after Marcell Dareus laid a massive blow to his shoulder while McCoy was trying to run the option. It wasn't as if he tripped over a camera wire or developed a stomach virus. He was tackled—and in football, a tackle can lead to an injury.

The injury of Colt McCoy was unfortunate for both Texas fans and Alabama fans because we didn't get to see Texas at their best, but it wasn't *luck*. Luck didn't cause the Alabama defense to smother the running game of the Longhorns, and it certainly didn't carry Trent Richardson and Mark Ingram into the end zone. In sports, as in life, you have to overcome adversity. Texas fought valiantly but they couldn't overcome the big hit that Dareus laid on their leader that night.

As Lorenzo reminds us, *"Marcel hit him good. I've seen quarterbacks get hit worse and stay in the game ... more than likely was a stinger. If he wanted to come back in, he could have come back in. It's the National Championship game. Regardless of if you're getting drafted or not, you can only win one National Championship and it was your last game in college. Nothing would have kept me out. Josh Chapman played with a torn ACL for eight weeks his senior year. So, a little stinger did the job? I don't know how that would keep anybody out of that game."*

Texas Longhorn fans may never discard their *luck* claim. That's okay, because Alabama football fans know better. Another reason why this is a myth is because there's no proof had McCoy played the outcome would have differed. Was he having a good first quarter? Yes. Does that mean he would have dominated the rest of the game with no struggles? No. Anyone who has watched Alabama play football under Nick Saban knows they usually start a little slower, adjust, and end up smothering opponents in the end. How many times have we seen an Alabama opponent blast into the first quarter full of emotion and hype? How many quick touchdowns and big plays have we witnessed against the Tide within the first few minutes of a game?

Does anyone remember when Alabama played #12 Florida in 2011? Florida scored with a deep passing play within seconds of the game beginning. The crowd went nuts! They were going to really take it to Alabama and sent a strong message via the pass—until reality settled in. Final: Alabama 38 Florida 10.

My point is if you hear the myth that McCoy would have played like Joe Montana the entire game, don't believe it. Alabama would have adjusted to their read option quickly with Saban behind the headset.

Another reason why this fantasy is told among the college football world is because backup quarterback, Garret Gilbert, found success on the Tide defense. The logic follows that if the backup found success, then the starter would have found even more. Again, this is all wishful thinking, but let's play that out for a minute.

Gilbert came into the game and did play well. There's no question about it. But Alabama did not prepare for him and became complacent once they gained a huge lead. That's also a trend we saw see earlier on in the Saban era. Once Alabama took the threat seriously, and adjusted to Gilbert's style of play, it was over. Due to that, and despite what the burnt orange wants to believe, there is no evidence McCoy would have fared better than Gilbert did that night in Pasadena.

How do I know? Because Gilbert still came up short. He didn't win the game. He was sacked and fumbled the ball. Alabama recovered and shortly after won the game.

Myth Busted

McCoy had a good first quarter till he was injured. There is no proof Alabama wouldn't have adjusted to his play and smothered him like they did Tebow. McCoy also didn't play defense. Gilbert still lost the game. One program flourished after that night. The other? Well, you know.

Myth #2

Alabama Didn't Deserve to Play in the 2011-2012 National Championship

Ah, yes—the good old *Alabama didn't deserve it* myth. While this story seems to pop up with any sports team that finds success, it's been stuck on Alabama with special attention. It's true Alabama needed help to reach the 2011 title game, but saying they didn't deserve to be there is a farce.

In 2011, Tuscaloosa was recovering from the tornado attack that had occurred there in the spring. The team was bonded with the community in restoration efforts, and they chose to dedicate the season to the storm victims and Tuscaloosa at large. That means they were determined to play hard and represent the "A" they donned on Saturdays even more than usual.

Alabama was loaded and ready that year—outside of an early season quarterback controversy. They had star running back Trent Richardson, a massive offensive line, and a defense that some consider the greatest ever in college football history. They tore through most of the schedule until they met rival LSU in what was deemed "The Game of the Century."

Alabama lost that game 9-6. The haters rejoiced. Alabama would not reach the National Championship, and all was right in the world. However, even though Alabama wouldn't win their division, they still found themselves in a rematch against LSU at the Sugar bowl. Based on people's reactions, it was a travesty equal to Watergate. How could this happen? Alabama had lost! They didn't do enough to get in. They hadn't earned that spot compared to the other one loss teams behind them. They didn't *deserve* it.

As the whining went on day after day in the media war rooms, this myth built into epic proportions. At that time, Virginia Tech and Oklahoma State were the front runners for the moaners who couldn't swallow the thought of Alabama in the title game. We need historical context to understand why this thinking was flawed to being with.

The ACC was terrible that year. The Hokies had lost to Clemson and were trying to fight their way back into the picture. What's bewildering is the hypocrisy of the pundits who claimed Alabama *didn't deserve it*, but they didn't mind boosting a Virginia Tech team who had lost to a lower ranked opponent in a weaker conference. But, that's how it goes with myths. People forget those pesky things called details in order to build a narrative so their preconceived bias can play out the way they want it to. Remember, however, the talking heads will tell you they are just stating the facts.

Oklahoma State was also a one loss team. Their loss was inexcusable. They lost to an Iowa State team that Hoover High could have hung with that season. Yes, they won the Big 12. Yes, they beat Oklahoma. No, it doesn't mean they deserved it more than Alabama did. Alabama lost to a #1 ranked LSU team in overtime. Alabama played in the Southeastern Conference. Alabama also had cupcakes like Oklahoma State did, but the Cowboys couldn't finish theirs off in order to make it without dispute.

'BAMA FOOTBALL MYTHS

Are we honestly supposed to believe that losing to Iowa State was not as bad as losing to LSU? Really?

As the sports world continued to sell this myth, people were even rationalizing Houston being placed in the game above Alabama. After all, they had defeated UAB and Georgia State. They had Keenum and company operating a modern-day air raid offense. They ripped the conference—whatever the name of it was—up that year. The hype was building. Emotions were running high. You could hear people chanting…*Houston! Houston! Houston!*—until they lost to Southern Miss in their conference title game and ceased to exist anymore once Sumlin bolted for greener pastures.

I hope a picture is starting to form. Did Alabama really not *deserve* to be in the title game, or did people sell that myth because they didn't want to see Alabama in the title game? I think the question answers itself. People don't like for one team to win a lot. It's human nature. Instead of admitting this about themselves, they would rather find something to blame outside of themselves. Hence, let's blame Alabama for wanting to play for a title and not advocating for other teams to take their place. How dare they?

But what is the greatest piece of evidence that Alabama deserved to play in the title game? They won it! It's kind of hard to say they didn't *deserve* it when they *won* the title game by 21 points. LSU had barely been scored on all year, and Alabama absolutely dismantled them—mentally and physically. I've heard Mike Gundy, the Oklahoma State head coach, claim they would have won it too. As a matter of fact, he said this recently:

"We would have played LSU and won," Gundy said in a lengthy interview with ESPN's Chris Low. "They were an overload-the-box, man-to-man team on defense, and you could not play our team in man that year. We were too good. That still bothers me, that we didn't get a shot. And if the system was set up like it is now, we would have been in the playoffs. I guess those things don't drive me as much. I love for our kids to have success, don't get me wrong. But I don't dwell on it like I used to."

Notice how Gundy says, *"we didn't get a shot."*

Yes, you did. You had a shot and blew it against Iowa State. You choked. Stop perpetuating the myth, Coach Gundy. Alabama deserved is as much as your team did. It wasn't the system that did it. You didn't fall victim to a tyrannical BCS computer. You didn't make it because you blew your opportunity.

Myth Busted

Alabama did deserve to be there. They had a difficult schedule. They didn't lose to a cupcake or play in a weak conference. They lost to a Number One ranked rival in overtime. They were immensely talented. They had just as much of a resume as anyone else. They won the title game by a blow out and went on to win more championships after that. The only thing they don't *deserve* is the unwarranted criticism they receive for the 2011 championship.

Myth #3

Alabama Always Plays a Weak Schedule

The myth of Alabama's *weak schedule* has gained substantial steam in recent years. Once the critics realized they could no longer wait for Alabama to miss the playoffs, they turned to attributing its success to scheduling. While it's true that Alabama does play some cupcakes here and there, they also play quality opponents year in and year out. Therefore, I'll enjoy busting this myth once and for all. I'll enjoy it because I'm tired of hearing it. This myth belongs in the same category as Bigfoot, Santa Clause, and the Warren Commission report.

There's not much reason to waste time in chopping this fairytale down from its foundation. Despite people crying about Alabama's weak schedule, the numbers tell quite a different story:

The following list reflects Alabama's strength of schedule from 2009-2018 at the end of each season:

2009-10: #5
2010-11: #10
2011-12: #24
2012-13: #19
2013-14: #38
2014-15: #4
2015-16: #1
2016-17: #1

2017-18: #29
2018-19: #22

There you go. From 2009-2018 Alabama has had a *hardest schedule* rating in the Top 10 five times. Two different times they had the hardest schedule in the country. Both of those years they played in the National Championship, splitting the series with Clemson. As for the other years, the whole *they don't play anybody* myth crumbles when you examine the details a little closer. Outside of Alabama's Top 10 finishes in schedule strength are four Top 30 finishes. Compare that 10-year stretch to anyone in the country and you will see that the Tide hasn't had anything easy while chasing and maintaining their dynasty.

As a matter of fact, in the 2017-18 and 2018-19 seasons Alabama tried to schedule challenging games to open the season years in advance. Playing against Florida State in Atlanta wasn't a cake walk. They fought the Tide tough until their starting quarterback, Deondre Francois, was injured towards the end of the game. Florida State was a Top Five team at the time Alabama played them, but they went on to have a disappointing season.

Fans who claim Alabama didn't play anyone forget that losing your starting QB at the beginning of the season can affect you. (No, it's not the same as losing him for three quarters, Texas fans). They also don't consider that Alabama is legendary for ruining people's dream seasons. The reason why I say that is because teams put everything they have into beating Saban and company. Once reality settles in and it doesn't happen, these teams march on to the bitter end—realizing they couldn't hang with the best. I see it year in and year out. Maybe it's Alabama PTSD for their opponents?

Louisville was also supposed to be a better match up for Alabama than the cake walk it turned out to be. Alabama scheduled them, confident that Petrino could put together a good team. It's important to recall that the previous year—before Alabama smoked them—they had a Heisman trophy winning quarterback in Lamar Jackson. They also were competitive in the ACC. Is it Alabama's fault that Jackson declared for the draft before they could play against him? Could Alabama control the garbage that Petrino put on the field the year they played them? Of course not!

Schools schedule teams years in advance. Nick Saban has scheduled some big-time opening games for the Tide since he's been there. There were all those Top 25 match ups against teams like Virginia Tech, Clemson, Michigan, Wisconsin, USC, West Virginia, and Penn State. The Tide also played regularly against highly ranked opponents in the SEC and in the playoffs/bowl system. The bottom-line is that Nick Saban and his crew don't cower from a difficult match up. This entire scenario about Alabama desiring a weak schedule is just pure fiction.

And by the way, why isn't Clemson's schedule an outrage? Is it because Wofford is a real contender? I don't see people upset that the Tigers are walking on easy street. I'm not upset either, because I understand that it doesn't change anything. Clemson is still Clemson. They are still a legitimate threat to win the championship year in and year out. It doesn't matter to me if they had one more Top 10 game because they would likely dominate that opponent too.

Alabama's schedule is so highlighted because people don't like them. I'm fine with that. I just want the them to admit it.

Myth Busted

Alabama has frequently had difficult, Top 25 opponents.

Their schedule has ranked in the top in difficulty five times in the last 10 years. They try to schedule difficult opponents, but they aren't responsible if those opponents don't live up to their ranking.

Myth #4

ALABAMA PLAYERS BUST IN THE NFL

There are flying unicorns, megalodons hiding in the Mariana Trench, honesty in Washington, and the myth that players from Alabama don't fare well in the NFL. Just as the *Neverending Story* was created as a mythical children's tale for entertainment, so was this story. I guess the old saying is true, *If you tell a lie long enough, people will believe it.*

The truth, which many 'Bama haters can't seem to handle, is found in the statistics. The numbers don't lie. Alabama is not only well represented in the NFL, they are becoming the nucleus of it. If you look around at the different positions, you'll see a wealth of talent who played under Coach Saban. There are stars like Julio Jones, Amari Cooper, Dont'a Hightower, Eddie Jackson, James Carpenter, Derrick Henry, and Marcell Dareus everywhere. Not to mention the others, the Riptide players, who work hard behind the scenes for their teams—they also are stacked up on the professional rosters.

The following statistics will clearly show how successful Nick Saban has been at producing NFL-caliber talent during his tenure at Alabama. Please close this book and exit the room if you cannot handle those facts. I realize it could be traumatizing to those who have *Alabama fatigue.*

"If the Alabama alumni on the offseason rosters of NFL teams were all on the same squad, 16 would have to be released in September to meet the league's regular-season roster limit. With rosters expanded to 90 slots in the offseason, 69 former Alabama players are in the NFL at a time when every team will have started the OTA portion of its offseason program by Tuesday."

Yikes! This means former Alabama players who turned professional could fill an entire NFL team roster all by themselves. They would even have to release 16 players to meet the league's limit. That's what you call a wealth of talent. But it isn't just talent that gets Tide players drafted. It's also the reputation, coaching, and work ethic they receive while enrolled in Tuscaloosa that earns them the necessary attention. While social media warriors and SEC hate-pundits recite this myth dutifully, NFL coaches salivate at the opportunity to evaluate a former Crimson Tide player.

"He has built a phenomenal program," Ravens coach John Harbaugh said of Nick Saban.

Harbaugh knows firsthand. "The thing you know about those Alabama guys is that football is important to them," Harbaugh said. "They understand the value of competing every day at practice and working hard in the offseason. They understand pressure and that you have to do things right, that there is a line, and you can't go below it if you want to be successful and be on the field. They know everything is earned. I don't think they come in with any sort of entitlement. To me, that's a credit to coach Saban."

That's all you really need to hear folks. This myth is about as strong as Tennessee football on Saturday morning once it's exposed. The numbers don't lie. The players don't lie. The coaches don't lie. Alabama is the epicenter of the NFL draft universe.

Addressing a final point that drives this myth is the *bust* label people like to toss around. "Alabama players bust" you hear. But is that true? Do a lot of Tide players bust in the NFL?

I don't think so. One must simply shift their perspective in order to understand this point. Has Alabama had some players bust? Yes, they have. Trent Richardson didn't work out. Eddie Lacy was short lived, though I wouldn't call him a bust. Rolando McClain had off the field issues that drove him out of the league. Who else is there that people would consider a bust? Not many.

When you have a mass number of players drafted from one team, you'll also have some disappointments along the way. The very fact that people sit back and mock a player from Alabama who doesn't translate well into the NFL just shows you how good they are to begin with.

Myth Busted

Alabama has players everywhere in the NFL. Coaches love to draft Alabama players. They could make their own NFL squad out of Crimson Tide players if they wanted to. There are hardly any busts to come out Tuscaloosa.

Myth #5

Auburn is on Alabama's Level

I remember watching the *Kick Six*. As Coach Saban called timeout and attempted to win the game with a field goal, my heart was filled with the anticipation of a modern day, *The Kick*. That didn't happen. The ball sailed in the air and landed in Auburn's arms. As Davis ran it all the way back, I drifted into an alternate universe filled with chips and soda. The sugar and salt were used to dull the pain of what I had just experienced.

My dreams were crushed. Alabama was on its way to a three-peat that year. Auburn was also a solid team. They had a great offense, but what they really had was a miracle persona that got them into the National Championship. I've witnessed it my entire football life. Auburn wins games through freakish circumstances.

The Kick Six? Yeah, it hurt. I'm sick of seeing it. I'm sick of hearing it. I'm sick of Auburn. However, I think a myth has been built across this country based on that one moment in time. The myth I speak of is that Auburn is a juggernaut that goes toe to toe with Alabama year in and year out. Hold on. I need to laugh. Okay, I can continue now.

Is Auburn a good football program? Yes, they are. They are a good little sister to Alabama. They do good for the state when they play Memphis and Purdue. Are they on the level of Alabama? No. They aren't even close to being on that level. Sure, Auburn occasionally has a magical moment where the ball bounces off ten defenders and lands in their hands in the end zone. They do win some big games here and there. They even beat Alabama—albeit infrequently. But this entire scenario about how they stand up against Alabama on behalf of the SEC is just a load of garbage.

They want people to believe that their wild west offense can't be stopped. They promote it because that's all they are: a glorified arena team. Auburn fans, you need to know something. Alabama players have bled, sweated, and worked their way to greatness. You have a Kick Six moment, and that makes you great? That's ridiculous! The truth is your program is built on hyped up Disney moments. You rely on emotion and big plays. You strive to beat Alabama with voodoo. Alabama is built on hard work and the infamous *process*. Alabama strives to win the National Championship, not just beat Auburn.

The myth that Auburn is on Alabama's level must be eradicated with the utmost force. It's not only dangerous for Alabama fans to believe, it's also toxic for Auburns fans to believe. Why? Because Auburn needs to wake up and accept their lot in the college football universe. It is only by admitting you are powerless over Alabama football that you can begin the road to recovery. The Gus bus ran out of gas years ago, and it's time to own that.

To truly debunk this theory, we need to look at the numbers:

Alabama leads the series 46-36-1. Yes, Auburn had their streak. But how many national titles did they win during that streak? They won a total of—zero. Speaking of national titles, Alabama has won 17 while Auburn has won two. Kick Sixes and miracles on the plains are wonderful bedtime stories, but at Alabama we produce championships.

So, is Auburn a con artist? I think so. They have been capable of pulling off a modern-day Wizard of Oz. They seem very important to college football because they sell people they are. They do it through cool Under Armour commercials and gimmicky offensive schemes. Yet, the result is usually the same: mediocrity that's only elevated if they can beat big brother once in a while.

Myth Busted

Auburn relies on magical moments and gimmicks to stay relevant. Auburn looks amazing two times a year. Auburn is Alabama's little sister. Auburn is statistically inferior to Alabama. Auburn strives to beat Alabama, while Alabama strives to win the National Championship.

And by the way, Auburn fans, for years you made life difficult for me. As I returned to school each year during the *streak* you were there. You already had that cheap pressed victory shirt on your back. (How you got that shirt so quickly is beyond me). You laughed and danced around the hallways. All was well in your world. I want to ask you, now that you have witnessed the Saban dynasty, how does it feel? All those years of beating us, and zero titles to show for it.

Alabama has won more titles under Coach Saban than you could even dream about. That's why, right here and now, I'm inviting you to come to the light. We will accept you as an Alabama fan. All you must do is apologize to Nick Saban for ever cheering for a team like Auburn, burn all your orange and blue clothing, and admit we are the superior program. What say ye?

Myth #6

NICK SABAN IS A TERRIBLE PERSON

In my last book on Alabama football, *The RipTide*, I spent significant time discussing what Nick Saban was like with his former players. While some will have you believe Saban is a tyrant who enjoys pushing people into the abyss, those who are close to him tell a different story. They paint the picture of a man who is intensely devoted to perfecting the details of his craft. They also testify that he is concerned about the future and current well-being of those around him.

So where does the *Nick Satan* myth come from? In my opinion, most of the time it originates in jealousy. Saban isn't sinless. He doesn't claim to be. He has had strained relationships during his career. Who hasn't? Yet, the media tends to exaggerate those normal life occurrences into something bigger than reality. If he gets upset and chews someone out on the sideline, all the sudden he is a terrible abuser of power who needs to be humbled. If he gets on to a player in a tough manner, he's abusing the kids. If someone gets injured it's because Saban works them too hard. It goes on and on.

Yet, that's not what his players think. They are the ones who know him better than you or I do. They are the ones who have toiled underneath his leadership. Let me give you some examples:

"I would say that he is a perfectionist. I had the opportunity

to see both sides of this because I played for the Patriots as well. I'm a football historian, so I kind of see the background of where Coach Saban came from. He's a very smart guy. He has a master's in psychology so he is probably one of the most intense mental coaches, but he does it with his degree so he really knows what he's doing. Everything he does is calculated. I wouldn't say everything is premeditated because it almost sounds criminal (laughs), but for him every part of the process of the program is thought through."

Lorenzo Washington, former defensive lineman

First, I would say if you go to Alabama, Coach Saban is going to make you a better person on and off the field. He will help you with your career after Alabama. Whether you play football or not, he's going to be there to help you. If you want to win and compete for the National Championship; if you want to play for the best in the business and be prepared for life in whatever it is you do; that's what Alabama offers and what he will teach you. That pretty much says it all."

Parker Philpot, former defensive back

"He wants you in shape mentally and physically. A lot of people think the game of football is a physical game, but it's just as much mental as it is physical. So, he puts you through conditioning tests and strength and conditioning programs that really bring you to your mental breaking point. When it's over you breathe that sigh of relief because he tends to make practice more intense than what you would see in a real game. For instance, we run like 100-120 plays per practice, when the average number of plays run per game is 70 or 80.

Practices are definitely more intense than the game. A lot of times we're not trying to beat each other up, and hurt each other so we can be healthy for the game. But mentally those practices are a lot more strenuous. He puts us in situations where you're almost set up to lose, so he definitely has that part of the game figured out."

Eryk Anders, former linebacker

As you can see these players don't tell a story of oppression and abuse. They tell a story of an amazing experience they had with a historic coach. I think some of the lesser known stories about Saban are the ones where he has helped people develop careers and aided them with their personal struggles in life. The media doesn't seem interested in promoting those moments. They would rather talk about how he doesn't enjoy the parade after a championship, or about how Lane Kiffin thinks he knows better when it comes to running a program.

Nick Saban knows what he's doing. He doesn't need to defend himself. He certainly doesn't need me to defend him. I just know the myth of Saban being abusive needs to be eliminated.

I think a lot of the criticism Saban gets is unwarranted because people don't understand his mentality. Overachievers don't like mediocre people, and mediocre people don't like overachievers. That comes from the mind of Nick. When he, on a *60 Minutes* interview, being criticized as being too hard on people, Saban retorted that very sentiment through that logic. He has high standards. He wants to win. He doesn't just want to win on the scoreboard. He wants to win every moment of every day.

He can keep hard working, Type A personalities around him without having to prove himself. Most people are too insecure for such a thing, but Saban cares more about being successful than he does stroking his own ego. He can take some of the most talented players in the country and mold them into disciplined warriors who seek and destroy their opponents through his process. He has been able to evolve over time with his coaching. He doesn't have so much pride that he always must stick with his system. He learns from others and adapts to the current landscape of college football.

Considering all of that, I think it's safe to say Coach Saban isn't what a lot of people think he is. Has he made mistakes in his career? Yes, he has. He always gets back up, learns from them, and adjusts for the greater good. He's the greatest college football coach of all time. I suppose you don't get that title without some baggage, true and false, along the way.

Myth Busted

Coach Saban is loved by his players. Coach Saban has a different mentality than most people. Coach Saban can surround himself with Type As without feeling threatened. Coach Saban can humble himself and change.

Coach Saban has made mistakes—but so have you.

Myth #7

Alabama Hasn't Had a Legit Quarterback Since Tua Tagovailoa

If you hear people talk about Alabama's quarterback history, you'll hear negativity with a cherry on top. I'll admit that Alabama isn't known for producing great quarterbacks, but the myth doesn't say *great*—it says *legit*.

We know historically that the Crimson Tide hasn't had a Peyton Manning or Tim Tebow. Until Tua, they haven't solely relied on a quarterback's arm to win a championship. Yet, the myth that none of them were legit outside of Tua simply isn't true.

Let's dig into the past a little bit for further clarification. I'm going to list my top five greatest QB's in Alabama history. Of course, this is my opinion. I realize many might disagree, but that's okay. We will have some fun with it.

1. Tua Tagovailoa
2. Joe Namath
3. Bart Starr
4. AJ McCarron
5. Blake Sims

Joe Namath, Tua, and Bart Starr are givens. However, because AJ hasn't panned out to be a stud in the NFL, I feel like he's been forgotten. McCarron was a legitimate quarterback in college. There's no question about it. He's a three-time National Champion. He's a Maxwell Award winner. He's a Johnny Unitas Golden Arm Award Winner. He's a First Team All-American. Not to mention he also was the 2013 Heisman trophy runner-up. That is an impressive resume.

That's why I consider AJ with the greats. He isn't just *legit*. He is a historic college football player. Now, I can hear some people retorting right now in their head. "He was surrounded by talent." That's true. Why is that a strike against him? He still had to distribute the football to them. He had to run the offense. He had to live under the pressure of guiding Alabama into contention year in and year out. What other quarterback in college football had to do that in the modern era?

AJ also had heart. He wore the program on his sleeve and willed his team to numerous victories. I recall when he led Alabama down the field against LSU, finally connecting with TJ Yeldon for the go-ahead touchdown in Death Valley. I also cannot forget when AJ systematically picked LSU's defense apart in the National Championship game at the Sugar Bowl. If you don't believe me, go review the tape for yourself. He had attitude, class, work ethic, and a passion for the game. More importantly, when it comes to busting this myth, he had the numbers to back up his legitimacy as a quarterback.

The other *legit* name on the list is Blake Sims. Sims, who was a backup running back for most of his career, took over the reigns at quarterback once AJ graduated. This was an incredible feat considering Sims was filling those shoes while fighting off the highly touted transfer Jake Coker. Sims had a rocky start against West Virginia in his opener, but he ended up having a killer season for Saban and company.

Who can forget the times when Blake would drop back and throw a 50-yard bomb to Amari Cooper? I remember when he out gunned Florida, Tennessee, Auburn, and Missouri. In a short period of time, he went from a scout team running back to leading Alabama to an SEC title and a number one spot in the playoffs. If that isn't impressive, or legit, I don't know what is. Sims also had the numbers to back his story up. He could read a defense, had blazing speed, and could torch the defense with his deep ball. Those skills eventually added up for Sims. He broke the single season passing record for Alabama. In one season he threw for almost 4,000 yards. He had nearly 30 touchdowns against 10 interceptions. He was a true underdog story, and his path to success came through a road less traveled. In short, he was legit.

Let's not also mention National Championship winning quarterback, Jake Coker. He was tough as nails and could throw under duress. The Alabama system isn't always built for a quarterback to achieve gushing statistics. Derrick Henry was the focus of the offense the year Jake was there. Let's not forget, however, that there were moments where Coker made crucial throws in order for Alabama to win it all. He was a legitimate quarterback. If you don't believe me just ask Ole Miss, Texas A & M, Auburn, Florida, Michigan State, and Clemson.

Myth Busted

Alabama hasn't had many great quarterbacks, but they have had legitimate ones. AJ McCarron and Blake Sims had the numbers and accolades to back that claim up. They both led their teams to titles, played on title teams, and set records along the way. Do I also need to again mention Bart Starr and Joe Namath? They are Super Bowl winning legends, my friends.

Myth # 8

The Officials Cheat for Alabama

Anytime a team has had success like Alabama has, people scramble for excuses as to why that happens. It can't be attributed to talent, hard work, coaching, or anything internal. The haters cannot give credit where it's due, so they must find a conspiracy as to why Alabama is winning.

Take for instance the illogical stance people take when Alabama wins a big game. They tend to tell everyone, "the referees wanted Alabama to win, so they gave them all the calls." As ridiculous as this myth is, let's play it out for the sake of truth.

Since Nick Saban has arrived at Alabama, he is 141-21. He has won six Southeastern Conference titles and five national titles. That's all been accomplished over an 11-year span. So, if you believe the conspiracy theorists, Alabama has had assistance from the referees in winning those games for more than a decade. Forget the fact that the referees come from differing conferences at times. Those pesky facts don't matter. They have been cheating for the Tide in a nationwide plot to help them become the greatest dynasty of all time.

I don't know why they didn't cheat for Alabama in the games they lost. I don't know where they were when we played Clemson. Maybe Coach Saban couldn't pay them anymore? Maybe they caught *Alabama fatigue* too? Who knows? I think you're catching my drift.

Consider the following statistics from an article posted on this topic:

"According to TeamRankings.com, Alabama's opponents had the fewest penalties called against them in 2016, ranking No. 128 out of 128 teams.

Specifically, opponents were flagged just 58 times for 471 yards. It's the fewest of any Alabama team during the Saban era (since 2007) without even factoring in the number of games.

Incidentally, Clemson was No. 4 on that list.

If Alabama's opponents had been called for their average number of penalties, there would have been 86.8 flags thrown.

Some of that can be credited to referees swallowing their whistles when games were no longer in doubt, and that happened with Alabama. The average score of its games was 38.8-13.

Additionally, Alabama made more penalties than it usually does, which was partly due to numerous false starts by the offensive line. It had 86 penalties for 660 yards after having 89 for 835 in 2015 with another first-year starter at quarterback.

Previously, no Saban team at Alabama tallied more than 69 flags (2009 and 2014).

However, in its two College Football Playoff games, the Crimson Tide's opponents were both flagged just three times (those declined and offsetting penalties excluded).

Washington was called for a false start, illegal substitution and unsportsmanlike conduct. Clemson's were for roughing the passer, a personal foul and a false start. The Tigers played the entire second half with getting a penalty."

Translation: The Myth isn't true when you line it up beside the numbers and logic. As it usually goes with conspiracy theories, the story crumbles once you start paying attention to the details. Thus, the unusual craving to blame the referees for Alabama's success is silly. It belongs with Humpty Dumpty, the Russian hoax, and the thought that the Big Ten is a legitimate conference.

Alabama wins because they are good. It's that simple. Do referees miss calls? Yes, they do. It all evens out though, because every team suffers bad calls by the end of the season. Ironically, when a fan argues that Alabama gets all the calls, they are saying their team should. In that, they wouldn't mind getting some calls for own team at the expense of their opponent. Their hypocrisy knows no bounds!

And come on guys—really? Are we going to blame the zebras for their incompetency? Tell me what referees haven't missed calls in a game? Does it mean they are a part of an international conspiracy, or does it mean they're human? How do you think Miami felt about the pass interference call in the end zone? I know you guys remember that travesty. My point is that since the beginning of sports being officiated, officials have blown calls. It usually evens out, so relax.

I think, considering all the information at hand, the trolls should maybe write the zebras an apology letter. They need to admit they were wrong about accusing them of cheating for Alabama. They need to simply express how they have come to realize their team gets a lot of penalties due to poor tackling, shoddy coverage in the defensive backfield, and an overall lack of conditioning. They need to admit the tape shows Alabama consistently wins games on the defensive and offensive lines—not by holding—but by pure force. They need to confess their coach and his game plan are systematically outmaneuvered through hard work and study. They need to evaluate that while their coach was on ESPN complaining about how life isn't fair, Nick Saban was traveling the country out-recruiting them. Man, this even hurts me to write this. It must hurt those who want to blame the referees even more.

Myth Busted

The logic and numbers prove Alabama wins a lot of games because they are great. They don't need the referees' help since most of their wins come through blow outs. Where were the referees in the games Alabama lost? Also, how do the referees pull off this conspiracy to help Alabama win? Do they all meet in a bunker and decide they will do what it takes to help the Crimson Tide? Are they putting their careers at risk in order to help Nick Saban win another ring? Have they done this for over a decade now? How are they able to convince everyone to be quiet about it? Maybe Alabama just out works everyone and gets more calls because your team is tired.

Myth #9

Alabama Pays Its Players

Man, did you see Julio Jones driving his hummer to school? He had a Rolex on and a Gucci suit. He had alligator skin boots and diamond earrings. Where did he get the money for all of that? What about Tua? You can't tell me the University didn't pay him to come to Alabama! His family moved here and Saban personally bought them a house. Where did he get the money for that stuff if Alabama didn't pay him? What agent is lurking behind the scenes, funneling these guys the hard cash it takes to live such lavish lifestyles?

That's the ridiculousness I've heard from people when it comes to Alabama football acquiring talent. *They pay their players* is a well-told tale. Never mind the fact that there's no proof of this. No one can produce a shred of evidence it has happened. The University would be in big trouble if they could. Outside of some text books issues and hearsay, Alabama has stayed relatively clean under Nick Saban. Those who have developed Alabama fatigue can't fathom that happening, so they create fairytales about players receiving illegal benefits.

"Everyone does it." I hear that line of reason presented as evidence that *"we know"* Alabama cheats by paying their players. Can you imagine using that logic in a court of law in order to prove something? *Your honor, we know Dan McCheesburger*

committed this crime because "everyone does it." The Judge might pass out or develop a hernia if his brain had to process such foolish reasoning. And yet, for some odd reason, people believe this myth wholeheartedly.

It seems to me the reason people believe this is the same reason they believe the other myths. They just cannot admit Alabama does things better than their team does. It hurts them to confess that. Alabama attracts top-tier players because they are a top-tier program with top tier-facilities and a top-tier coach. It's that simple.

Now, if an agent or booster does something shady behind the scenes, that's not Nick Saban's fault or even the University's fault. The program will be the one to pay the price with sanctions from the NCAA, but the perpetrator usually walks away without any punishment.

That's what people don't seem to understand. Just because a player gets paid or does something illegal doesn't mean the coaches and staff at the University were in a bunker somewhere controlling that plot. As a matter of fact, Coach Saban and his staff have programs the players walk through that educates them about the danger of receiving illegal benefits while enrolled in the University. So, as people build this conspiratorial thinking in their minds, ask yourself if it really makes sense?

If someone says they *know* Alabama pays their players, ask them how they know it? Who's paying the players? Coach Saban? Terry Saban? Big Al? Eli Gold? It doesn't make sense when you begin to play it out on paper. Yet, this is human nature isn't it?

Take for instance, there are people who passionately believe 9/11 was an internal conspiracy committed by our government. As an old friend, Gus Russo, points out: we should ask them who they mean when they say *government*. George Bush? The Republicans? The Democrats? The FBI? The CIA? The Supreme Court? These guys can barely get a bill passed together, much less build an international conspiracy in the modern age without getting caught.

That's how it goes with the whole *Alabama cheats* myth. Just take the time to really sit down and focus on that claim. It falls apart. The house of cards crumbles.

What's left is the cold hard truth that Nick Saban is a recruiting genius. He consistently outworks those around him. Kids want to play for him. They want to complete for championships. They want him to help them develop their skills and train them to become professionals. They trust him with their future. They know he can get them to the NFL. That's what the allure is.

Myth Busted

Nick Saban doesn't need to cheat in recruiting because of his track record. There's zero proof Alabama pays their players. The University or program usually aren't responsible if a player receives illegal benefits. You must ask yourself, "who is the one paying the players?" You also must ask yourself how people know they are getting paid.

Myth #10

Alabama Fans are the Worst

"*I don't mind the team, I just can't stand their fans*". Ah, yes, this one. This is one statement I just can't tolerate. I've noticed that it usually comes from people who root for teams that lose a lot. Those teams' fans are deemed humble and hopeful, while successful teams' fans are arrogant and unreasonable. I suppose that myth seems true until you start probing it further.

The truth is Alabama fans can be arrogant. All of this winning does go to our heads. I'll admit that. I like to talk trash with the best of them. I do find joy in beating rivals and winning championships. I rub it in.

I believe you would too. If your team was successful like Alabama, you would jump on this wagon as quickly as possible. Don't try to sell me because someone's team is garbage that means their fans are somehow *cool*. It's not cool—it's sad.

The only reason they are viewed as cool is because they have nothing to boast about. In a desperate attempt to grasp relevancy, they must turn their attention towards the fandom of successful programs. I get that. I really do. I honestly try to restrain myself from ragging poorer programs too much. Well—sometimes. What I can't stand is when a program is losing, and they rejoice when Alabama loses too.

When Alabama loses, I get calls, voicemails, social media

messages, texts, and even strangers blissfully coming to me to tell me how happy they are we lost. That's fine. I know it satisfies the insecurities of other fans temporarily. What I don't understand though, what I can't swallow, is how you talk trash about Alabama and your team has already been beaten by them.

When you do that, you prove my point. If you're going to talk trash to an Alabama fan when they lose, what would you do if your team was winning? Yes, you get what I'm saying here. You would be arrogant too.

I recall this debate I've had with Texas fans. In the early to mid-2000s, when they were a top-tier program, I remember their arrogance. They talked trash. They were cocky. They enjoyed smashing opponents. However, when they started losing and crying about Colt McCoy, they turned around and accused Alabama fans of being *The Worst*.

I suppose that's the way it goes. If your team wins, you will talk trash. If they lose, you will accuse other teams of talking too much trash. If your team wins, you will be arrogant. If they lose, you will have a forced humility. No matter the case, please don't kid yourselves, my fellow college football fans. You have a trash-talking beast inside you who's chomping at the bits to be released behind a keyboard once your program starts dominating like Alabama. You will show no mercy once your team finally rebuilds.

In the final analysis, Alabama fans aren't worse than any other fan base. They just have something to boast about right now. You aren't any different than us. One day your team's fan base, if you're fortunate, will have the opportunity to prove that statement true.

I would like to end this myth buster by quoting Alabama superfan, and journalist, Stan J. Griffin:

'BAMA FOOTBALL MYTHS

"Alabama fans are arrogant and rightly so. It is the greatest college football program of all time and the success lends its fans and followers to be very proud, although there are many who probably cross the line of being obnoxiously so (myself included). If you grow up in this state and especially Tuscaloosa and you've supported the school in however many ways, whether it be going to games, buying merchandise or just supporting them with all your heart, you can definitely say it's your program."

Well said Stan!

Myth Busted

Alabama fans aren't any different than any other fanbase. They just have more of a reason to boast right now because of the overall success of the program. If other programs had the same success, their fans would become *the worst* also. It's easy to be humble when it's forced upon you. As former fullback Jalston Fowler says about Alabama fans, "It's because they're very passionate about football. Football means a lot to them and even just losing a game is not Alabama's culture. They're used to winning every game and if you lose a game it's upsetting. The fans expect you to do big things every year and they live for it. They're actually diehard fans."

Myth #11

Alabama didn't Deserve to be in the 2017 Playoff

The year is 2017. The setting is Jordan Hare Stadium. Alabama has been upset by little sister Auburn. Their dreams of an undefeated season have evaporated. Their SEC championship destiny is gone. The program is in shambles. The defense is decimated. The dynasty is in utter ruination. Nick Saban is tail spinning towards hip surgery, and his golf game is now mirroring Charles Barkley's. Okay, it wasn't that bad—but it was bad.

After that loss questions were swirling around the college football universe. As in 2011, critics were already pitching a fit about how Alabama didn't deserve a shot at the title after a loss. "They shouldn't be in the playoffs without winning their conference!" That was the battle cry of the northern media. How dare someone put Alabama in the playoff? No one really believed the Tide wasn't one of the best four teams in the country, but they acted like it. They claimed Ohio State, who had won the big ten, deserved it more than Alabama.

Notice they didn't claim Ohio State was the better team. It was clear they weren't. Rather, what they said was the playoff spot should be determined by who earned it. Never mind the fact that the entire playoff system was built to put the four best teams in, regardless of people's feelings. People wanted Ohio State in, and they demanded the decision was made quickly. They even wanted Central Florida, North Dakota State, and Locust Fork High School in before they wanted Alabama to get a crack at it. It wasn't fair. They couldn't allow another year of good ole undeserving Alabama to win the playoffs. It would be a travesty of injustice!

Yet, there was Ohio State. They were a team who had been systematically dismantled by unranked Iowa— beaten by 31 points, 55-24.

"But they beat Wisconsin!" cried the detractors.

In the words of the late Chris Farley, "Well, la-de-da." It was never about who won the conference championship, and who didn't. It wasn't about who deserved it more, and who didn't. It wasn't about people's feelings, or their preconceived bias rooted in Crimson hate. It was always about who were the best four teams in the country.

No one in their right mind believed Alabama wasn't one of those teams. That's why the chairman of the playoff committee had this to say when it came to choosing Alabama for the playoff:

"The committee's conclusion that Alabama is the fourth-best team in the nation was widespread and strong. It was unequivocal," the selection committee's chairman, Texas Tech Athletic Director Kirby Hocutt, said Sunday afternoon."

One of issues with the *they didn't deserve it* myth is it's based on perception. That's all it is. It isn't rooted in facts or in a working knowledge of how the selection committee works. The reason why people wanted you to believe Alabama shouldn't get in is because they didn't want Alabama to get in in the first place. Its nothing more than that. It was insane how many

Ohio St. and Central Florida fans there were the week after Alabama lost to Auburn. I never would have guessed half of the country rooted for those teams. You would have thought those people would sacrifice their lives for those programs by the way they campaigned on their behalf.

The Alabama hate is real folks. It's an amusing case study into human psychology if you ask me.

The ultimate and greatest rebuttal for the *they didn't deserve it* myth is found in the same rebuttal for the 2011 debate. Alabama went on to win the entire playoff as the four seed. After slapping Clemson around in the semifinal, the Tide went on to win a miraculous title game against fellow SEC foe Georgia.

We all know what happened. With Jalen Hurts struggling, Coach Saban made the switch at halftime to freshman phenom Tua Tagovailoa. Tua went on to flex his arm strength and field vision, eventually winning the championship in overtime, via a deep connection with DeVonta Smith for a touchdown. Thus, the legend of Tua was born and Alabama proved their worthiness by hoisting the trophy once more.

Not that Alabama needed to prove it. They already proved it during the season by being one of the best four teams in the country. The title victory simply proved they were the best team in the country. The committee had made the right choice. Alabama sat atop the college football world as the undisputed champion once again.

Myth Busted

Alabama was better than Ohio State. Alabama was one of the best four teams in the country. To say *they didn't deserve it* isn't true because the playoff system is based on who the four best teams in the country are. It isn't based on who people think deserves it. Alabama went on to win the playoff, further solidifying the committee's decision to put them in the playoff in the first place. Silly rabbits—tricks are for kids.

Myth #12

Alabama Claims too many Championships

I'm going to be real with you on this point. Alabama does use a little liberty in claiming some of their national titles. Yet, what you don't hear when this myth pops up, is that they could easily claim more if they chose to do so. The truth is Alabama has a lot of National Championship titles. Take Coach Thomas and Wallace Wade out of the picture and Alabama is still sitting there with 12 titles. They have that reputation because the program is a walking dynasty.

Bear Bryant dominated the college football landscape for decades. Behind the houndstooth brim was a recruiting machine that gobbled up victories at will. Alabama's dynastic force under The Bear was unmatched until Nick Saban came to town. Imagine that scenario? One school has the luxury to debate who the greatest college football coach of all time is—and both candidates are from that very school.

That's why it's silly to nitpick Alabama over their title claims. If you want to take away a couple of championships because that makes you feel better, then so be it. However, even when you do, they still are the most dominate program of all time. There's not a question about that in my mind. It's not just the titles that create my confidence in that statement. It's the way they have won them, with physical defense and strategic coaching.

'Bama Football Myths

"The total number of National Championships for the Crimson Tide varies according to the Associated Press and the NCAA. Alabama claims they have won 17 National Championships, including titles in 1925, 1926, 1930, 1934, and 1941 before legendary Alabama head coach Bear Bryant took over. The confusion and debate among these early titles centers around the polling and ranking systems for those respective years. Alabama claims it has won national titles in 1925, 1926, 1930, 1934, 1941, 1961, 1964, 1965, 1973, 1978, 1979, 1992, 2009, 2011, 2012, 2015 and 2018."

That's not even to mention the 1992 National Championship team. You know, the one led by Coach Stallings. They had a defense that's considered one of the strongest units to ever be assembled in Tuscaloosa. They dominated Miami when people thought they didn't have a chance. They did it the 'Bama way. They were physical. They were talented. They were well-coached. That's how Alabama is known to be. It's the standard.

Nick Saban didn't create the winning culture at Alabama. He revived it. He even took it to new heights. Bear Bryant, Stallings, and many more had already created that culture years in advance. It was the desire of the University, after years of mediocrity in the early to mid-2000s, to reclaim that passion by hiring a coach like Nick Saban. This is why Alabama acquired him: to win titles. He hasn't disappointed.

Even if you want to discredit some of Coach Bryant's titles, Coach Saban still has won more of them at Alabama than most programs have throughout their entire existence. Strip it all away outside of him, and you would still be left with Alabama claiming five titles outright. If you wish to borrow some of the claims for your program, please write the University of Alabama or the NCAA and see what they can do to help you.

What's entertaining is that people even care enough to try to get some title claims removed. Why do they do that? Are they moral crusaders who want to right a historical wrong? I don't think so. The reason they are so interested in this topic is because—the Alabama hate is real.

When it's all said and done, Coach Saban could leave Tuscaloosa with seven championships under his belt. Whether you think the titles are legitimate or not, you cannot deny Alabama is a title producing machine. They just keep collecting them with no remorse. That's how it's always been, and that's how it will always be.

Myth Busted

Alabama could give away some of their titles and still be the greatest program of all time. Alabama has had two dynasties, with two of the greatest coaches to ever grace the sideline. Alabama could claim more titles if they wanted, so be happy they don't.

Myth 13

NICK SABAN PUSHES ASSISTANTS AWAY

No, he doesn't. Assistant coaches tend to leave the program because they either obtain a better job offer, or they cannot endure Saban's grueling work ethic. I think of Lane Kiffin. He was a tremendous coach during his tenure at Alabama. His offensive schemes, along with his ability to elevate players like Blake Sims and Jalen Hurts, were impressive. Yet, something soured towards the end of his stay there. He started forgetting that Saban had ripped him out of college football purgatory. He became irritated with *the process* that Nick is known to implement, and he expressed it every chance that he could.

After he landed his job at Florida Atlantic, he started sticking the knife to his former boss via the media. He didn't mention how his job performance at Alabama was failing before he was fired. Saban was left with no choice but to let him go. What came next was sad to witness. Kiffin complained and critiqued Saban for how he treated him during his tenure there. He had a lot of excuses for many different things, but the truth is he just couldn't take it anymore and that's why he was booted. He wasn't made for Alabama.

Yet, outside of his attitude issues, his initial hiring says more about Nick Saban than anything else. Lane Kiffin was radioactive when Saban gave him a chance to coach again. He had failed stints at USC, Tennessee, and the Oakland Raiders. He was viewed as toxic, although I believe he was still growing as a person during those experiences. He was a young coach in whom Saban saw potential. He gambled on Kiffin and it paid off.

That's how Coach Saban is. Despite people perpetrating the myth that he pushes coaches away; the facts tell a different story. How many times has he gone out on limb, enduring a media blitzkrieg, to hire an outcast coach? Lane Kiffin is just one name among many. There was Steve Sarkisian, the former disgraced head coach who struggled with substance abuse. Mike Locksley, who posted an abysmal record as a head coach before retreating to Tuscaloosa to revive his career. There's Major Applewhite, Mike Stoops, D.J. Durkin, and former Tennessee head coach, Butch Jones.

Nick Saban's ability to work with alpha males, those who have run their own programs, sometimes even competing against him, is incredible. He doesn't push coaches away. That's a bedtime story for those who need the door partially cracked. He redeems their career. He utilizes their skills. He helps them understand the tools they are missing by setting an example of football genius on their behalf. That's the truth.

So, where does this myth come from? I think it has a lot to do with our culture. In the older days, it was nothing to witness a coach scream at a player or assistant on the sideline. Now, ESPN plays it repeatedly as if it's an anomaly. Coach Saban is tough and demanding. There's no question about it. It doesn't mean, however, that he's a tyrant everyone is running from. That isn't a fair or honest assessment.

Take, for instance, how Sarkisian returned to Tuscaloosa. When he left after coaching one game in 2017, the media pounced on Saban. *Sark wanted out! Sark couldn't take the pressure! Sark was abused!* After all the banter, they are now silent in those claims since he made his return to coach underneath Saban. It's just another piece of evidence that people run to Saban and his program, rather than running away from it. Thus, the myth is effectively debunked.

Myth Busted

Coach Saban has been running a coaching rehabilitation center in Tuscaloosa for years. This proves the claim that he's pushing everyone away is false. Coaches run to him to achieve redemption for their careers. He has a proven track record to attract top coaches on his staff.

"No one produces more head coaches than Saban, recycled or not. Consider this ridiculous fact. Since 2015, here's the list of Alabama assistants who are now head coaches or have been hired to be head coaches after this season: Locksley (Maryland), Jeremy Pruitt (Tennessee), Mel Tucker (Colorado), Kirby Smart (Georgia), Billy Napier (Louisiana), Kiffin (Florida Atlantic) and Mario Cristobal (Oregon). That's more than twice as many future head coaches (eight) than Alabama losses (three) over the last four seasons. All that winning and polish will make even the most beat up coach look brand new."

Myth #14

KIRBY SMART IS THE NEXT NICK SABAN

I've read about this myth since the day Kirby left Alabama for Georgia. Kirby, who was a coordinator at Alabama from 2008-2015, took the Georgia job once it opened. Rumors about his backhanded tactics to steal recruits have swirled around message boards ever since. Some even say that Smart and Saban have a strained relationship due to how Kirby acted while transitioning out of Alabama. I think, from watching their interviews together, the tension is there. Yet, Smart could easily be frustrated by not being able to overcome his former mentor in a head to head battle.

It's not that Kirby isn't a great coach, because he is. The real issue is that people claim he's the next Nick Saban. I do understand why some would think that. He spent years learning under his tutelage. He knows how to run a program and recruit effectively. He has the attitude he needs to succeed. But, come on—he's Nick Saban 2.0? I don't think so. In the words of the late Dennis Green—if you want to crown them, then crown them—but they were who we thought they were.

Why is Kirby the next Nick Saban? Is it because he's won some games at Georgia? Is it because he almost beat Alabama? I saw a man get out-coached, if you ask me. Yes, Tua and Hurts made some clutch plays to deliver the victories for the

Crimson Tide, but Smart also withered in crunch times. I think he choked because he's *not* Nick Saban. You see, Coach Saban is one of a kind. You can implement and follow his plan, but you can't become an exact clone of the man. I think Kirby is finding that out the hard way.

Yes, he's got a great team. Yes, they could theoretically beat Alabama. That isn't the issue. The real issue is Nick Saban is the greatest college football coach of all time. He's won six national titles at two different schools. He's created a modern-day dynasty that's unrivaled in college sports history. Kirby Smart? What has he done to earn the thought that he's on that level?

The answer is nothing. It's a lot of hype. I would say Dabo Swinney is closer to Saban than Smart. That's yet to be seen. Remember that Nick Saban has proven that he can maintain his success over an extended period of time. Can Dabo do this for 10 years? Can Smart win title after title? We don't know. Only Nick Saban has accomplished it so far. That's why it's a myth to say Smart is even close to his former boss. And how many times have we heard a coach is coming for Saban's GOAT status? Les Miles, The Gus Bus, Urban Meyer, Bobby Petrino, and on and on. All of them have fallen by the wayside, becoming just another victim of Saban's dominance. Only Nick Saban is Nick Saban. Pepsi isn't Coke my friends.

Myth Busted

Kirby Smart has done nothing to be compared to Nick Saban. He can duplicate his program, but he'll never have the same natural giftings that Saban has. In the words of Ric Flair: "To be the man, you got to beat the man!"

Myth #15

WHEN ALABAMA LOSES THE DYNASTY IS DEAD

I don't even know where to begin with this myth. I think I'll start with the Ohio State loss in 2014. As Blake Sims pass failed to hit its target in the end zone, the pundits were already joyfully writing about Alabama's downfall. If Ezekiel Elliot ran right through the vaunted Alabama defense with such ease, what was really going on inside the locker room walls? Was hElliott that good? Was Alabama over-confident? Would they ever win another title?

Of course, Alabama came back in 2015 with a new quarterback in Florida State transfer, Jake Coker. They also would rely heavily on running back, Derrick Henry. All was going according to plan until Ole Miss came to town for a night game. After a series of events that belonged in the Twilight Zone, Alabama found themselves down and out early in the game. They turned the ball over like they were allergic to it. They had some freakish ball bounce all over creation before landing in a streaking Ole Miss player's arms for a touchdown. They didn't run Henry much. They started a nervous backup quarterback for reasons the universe may never understand.

Alabama fought back but lost the game. The media was drooling over the alleged death of their dynasty. Let's look at what some of the talking heads had to say after that upset:

"In life, you've got to be able to pivot, and I don't think Nick has been able to pivot particularly well," Cowherd said. "I always thought it was a boring dynasty. I liked USC's and Texas'. I sincerely believe it's over. They'll win a bunch of games, but it's over."

"It is," Klatt said in agreement. "Now they may get another class in here that may do something special because (Nick) recruits very well (but it's over). They have a Nick Saban problem at Alabama. They pay Kirby Smart and Nick Saban north of $8 million. And in the last 14 games they've given up 40 points four times. They haven't adjusted.

"This is what's so crazy—he's turned Alabama into an old Big Ten defense. It's a big, slow, lumbering defense. They've got some serious problems there. I think it's over. There are better programs out there right now than Alabama, and Ohio State is one of them."

Wow. He couldn't have been more wrong in his assessment. Alabama went on from there to destroy a Top 10 Georgia team the next week. After that, Saban angrily ripped the media about how they had buried the Tide after their Ole Miss loss. It was a beautiful thing to witness.

And yet, we've seen this same story perpetrated again and again. Every time Alabama loses a game, people claim that's the end for them. How about when Auburn beat Alabama via the Kick Six? How in the world would Alabama ever recover? What about when Johnny Manziel went off on Alabama? They had met their match! What about when LSU kicked their way to a victory in the Game of the Century? They broke Alabama's will! But, that's not what happened.

Alabama responded to all those losses with victories, sometimes resounding ones. After the Kick Six, the Tide went on to win two more National Championships. After Manziel did his thing, Alabama beat him in a rematch. After the LSU loss, Alabama smashed them in their backyard for another ring. Time and time again, I've heard the dynasty is dying after a loss. And time and time again, Alabama has responded with pure domination over a lengthy period of time.

This is a myth that needs to be buried underneath the sea with Atlantis. Give me a break. What's even more insane is this lie continues to grow. After the bludgeoning Clemson gave the Tide last season, people went at it again. They claimed it was over for Alabama because the mystique is gone after a loss like that. They fail to study the past.

Time will tell if that's true. After looking at the historical record I don't think it is.

Myth Busted

Alabama is the king of revenge games. Talking heads have repeatedly been wrong about where the program is headed. Alabama has proven that if Nick Saban is at the helm, the dynasty is secure.

Myth #16

Coach Saban Doesn't Discipline his Players

Nick Saban has gone soft. *The streets of Tuscaloosa aren't safe for the faint of heart. Alabama players roam them, seeking whom they may devour. The team is full of criminals, thugs, and mythical monsters. They are practically running a prison system at the football facilities. That's because Coach Saban lets his players get away with multiple crimes. The only reason it's so is because he cares more about winning than he does about the character of his program.*

While the paragraph above might sound extreme, that's what people believe when an Alabama player gets in trouble. Some people tend to enjoy it. They start out by magnifying the crime, and afterward seek to unify the media in making sure Nick Saban destroys them.

If an Alabama player commits any violation, these vigilantes ceremoniously grab their pitchforks and torches. Ah, the joy of discrediting Alabama and Nick Saban through a crime! As if that attitude isn't disturbing enough, the real sickness is found in how bloodthirsty people are to make sure he destroys a 19-year-old's life.

We want justice! Kick him off the team! Don't delay! Suspend them half the season. Let them self-destruct so they can learn.

Would these people treat their own children that way? No.

They claim they want Saban to severely punish his players in order to *help* the players learn from their behavior. Thankfully, Nick Saban cares more about their futures than what people in the media think of him. Anytime something occurs that requires discipline, he handles it internally without sacrificing the player for his own reputation. He has learned that response, according to his own biography, over a period of years—through trial and error.

In an age where justice is perverted through the lens of what an emotional mob desires, it's nice to see an old school coach lean on the side of grace. It isn't as if the players get away with anything. How would you like to face Nick Saban after you let him down? How would you like to face your brothers on the team knowing that you put yourself first? I'm sure it isn't an easy thing to do.

More importantly, the internal punishment isn't there for punishment alone. It's specifically tailored to correct the player's behavior.

"If we can change their behavior based on what we do, that would be the purpose of discipline. Discipline is not necessarily just punishment, which a lot of people view it that way. It's how do you change somebody's behavior, so they have a better chance to be successful.

"That's the way we've always done it. That's the way we always try to do it. That's the way I like to do it with my own children. I think that's the way most parents like to do it with their own children."

Nick Saban

When star tackle Cam Robinson had a run in with law enforcement, the media was infuriated Saban didn't suspend him immediately. Paul Finebaum, the controversial SEC pundit

'Bama Football Myths

who has followed Nick Saban for an extended period of time, challenged Saban on how he handled the situation. He basically accused Saban of putting winning before justice. Nick Saban wasn't thrilled with that accusation, so he went on to tell Finebaum this:

"I don't really care to answer the critics, because I'm going to do what's right for the players. If the players really did something that wrong, they would be charged with something."

Nick Saban

How refreshing is it to see a coach fulfill a promise he made while recruiting his player? When Nick Saban sits down to recruit a player, he promises them and their families he will give them his best. He doesn't back down from the media pressure. He protects them. He doesn't bend to the will of the public. He presses into the kid further. He has them engage in active community reform in order to correct the mistakes they have made. That's the mark of a great coach.

Now, there are exceptions where he's been burned. We all remember when he took on Jonathan Taylor, a player with domestic violence issues. After coming to Alabama, Taylor did it again, and Saban kicked him off the team. People slammed Saban for ever taking him in the first place. How did he respond?

"I think you learn from every experience, and we certainly learned some things from this one. I certainly don't condone that kind of behavior, especially when it comes to how females are treated, and that's something we try to create a lot of awareness for with our players, and we would certainly be very cautious about any player with any character problem, especially something like this, would be something that we would be very careful about in the future.

"But I will say this, we will continue to try to create

opportunities for players and try to help them be successful, and even in Jonathan Taylor's case, if there's anything we can do to help him overcome his issues and problem we will still certainly try and help him be successful. But right now the guy just can't be on our football team."

Nick Saban

Coach Saban went on to express sorrow over what happened but refused to apologize for giving the guy a chance. People look at that situation and wonder if Nick went soft, or if his ambition overtook him. They wonder if he took Taylor because of talent instead of refusing him for the sake of character. To answer those accusations, we must look at Saban's entire body of work when it comes to handling wayward players. He has had some difficult ones along the way, but he's been consistent in his reactions most of the time.

He usually handles the situation in-house. He doesn't many give details about them in the media. He allows the players to be involved in the discipline of the player as well. He responds according to the differing circumstances of the crimes committed.

That's why this is one the greatest myths in this book. People either think Nick Saban is too hard or too soft. They act as if they would do better in the situations he's put in when a player gets in trouble. Sometimes it's too much and he must kick them off the team, but most of the time even that is done out of love for the player. It's never vindictive.

Myth Busted

Nick Saban doesn't discipline players the way the media thinks he should. Because of this, the myth that he's soft or ambitious has been tossed around like a hacky sack. He cares more about his players than his reputation. Sometimes he must kick players off the team, but it isn't to destroy them. The proof in the success of his style of discipline is found in the pudding. Most of his players who get into trouble eventually turn it around and go on to successful careers.

Bonus Myth #17

NICK SABAN WAS A TERRIBLE NFL COACH

I wanted to take a moment to address this myth since Nick Saban is tied into the Alabama program. Sometimes, in order to discredit Alabama, people will belch out that Saban is a loser when it relates to the NFL. I don't really see the logic behind this argument, since he clearly is the best college football coach of all time. What does his stint in the NFL have to do with that?

I understand the motive that supplements this myth. People don't like successful programs. They become jealous. They move to discredit them. They cannot do this with facts, so they create stories. We've seen that process played out throughout this book. Considering that, it isn't a surprise they would try to grasp the wind through Coach Saban's time in the NFL.

Let's take a look at Nick Saban's NFL career. While he wasn't Bill Belichick, he wasn't terrible either. Historical context will be needed in order to understand why Coach Saban didn't make the play-offs as the leader of the Miami Dolphins.

"Saban took over a 4-12 Dolphins team, improving Miami to a respectable 9-7 and second-place AFC East finish in 2005. The next year his Dolphins went 6-10 before Saban decided to move on to Alabama. Saban took a four-win Dolphins team and squeezed nine victories out of them the following season. After Saban left the Dolphins, Miami fell to 1-15 the next year.

'Bama Football Myths

Saban's overall 15-17 record (a .469 winning percentage) is less than stellar, but it is far from awful. And it is more impressive considering the circumstances, which included an old defense, poor quarterback play, and an oft-suspended running back."

As we've previously discovered, historical context and statistics are rarely mentioned when a fable is crafted. So, here's Nick Saban. He's had history in the NFL. He's had success in the NFL as an assistant. He's mentored under one of the greatest NFL coaches ever. He's just won a title at LSU. He takes on the Miami Dolphins head coaching position. The team he took over was pure garbage. It was going to take time for him to rebuild a team that was prehistoric defensively and anemic offensively. He had to rely on stars like Jason Taylor and Zach Taylor, both aging superstars on their last legs. People think he was supposed to win the Super Bowl with that roster. But, is that fair? Did Belichick or Lombardi or Landry win a title as soon as they took their respective teams over?

Even worse, Nick Saban didn't have a quarterback. You can get away with that at the collegiate level, but in the NFL that's the surest path to destruction. After working out Drew Brees, the Dolphins opted to bring in gimping quarterback Daunte Culpepper. That didn't work out to well. People condemn Saban for not getting Drew, but at that time hardly anyone would touch him due to the nature of his shoulder injury.

Sure, Brees went on to win a Super Bowl in New Orleans, but when he took that team over no one actually believed that was going to happen.

Nick Saban takes over a 4-12 team and the next year they are 9-7? Then they go 6-10. He leaves because he decides he loves college football more. The next year the Dolphins go 1-15. Let me repeat. The year Nick Saban arrived the team was 4-12. The next two years they went 15-17. The year after he left, they went 1-15. I'll let you add those numbers up for yourself to see the difference he made on that franchise during the short period of time he was there.

When people say Saban was terrible, that's simply not the case. No one is saying he was great, but the numbers say he was good enough to almost have a .500 winning percentage with a depleted roster. Keep in mind that he was only there two years. What would have happened had he chosen to stay?

I don't blame Nick Saban for coming to Alabama when he did. How can I? Look at the results of what he did. Pete Carroll, who led Southern California and the Seattle Seahawks to championships, isn't considered as great as Nick Saban. Why is this so when he has won national titles and a Super Bowl? He isn't as great because what Nick Saban has done is legendary. He has become the greatest college football coach of all time. It's one thing to be considered a great coach. It's another thing to be considered the greatest coach of all time, no matter what level it's at.

Myth Busted

Nick Saban took over a Miami team that had an old roster, no quarterback, and a track record of losing. He turned them into a winning program within one season. He left for Alabama, not because he couldn't win, but because he knew where he belonged. His decision was the right one. Is it better to win a little at different levels, or to become a legend at one?

Myth #18

ALABAMA IS BORING TO WATCH

Alabama is so boring. The way they grind teams into dust, or blow opponents out with ease, is so lame. I want to see a high-octane offense that puts up 60 points a game. I don't care if they give up 50 points defensively while doing it. I am more impressed by gigantic stats than good defense and sound fundamentals. Will someone please come put me out of my misery if I must watch Alabama do it again this season? What's wrong with the playoff committee? Shouldn't they know how much of a snooze Alabama is for us? Why don't they put Baylor in front of Alabama? Who cares if their record isn't as good? They are cool.

That's the thought process I've witnessed from people who claim Alabama is boring. This is a myth indeed. It originates in a lack of understanding. Football isn't about who can score the most points. It isn't about who has the flashiest jerseys. You don't win games by building hip locker rooms and revealing them on ESPN while the players go nuts over it. Do those things if you want, but please understand that those things aren't winning anyone a championship. If winning is boring, then what is fun?

I also question if people who stir this pot actually watch Alabama play? What game are you guys watching that makes you think they are boring? Alabama is physical. They are smashmouth. They impose their will on the opposition week in and week out. How can you deny their greatness? I don't think you can, so all that's left is to claim they are boring. Well, who is exciting then? If you tell me Clemson is exciting, then I'll show you how similar they are to Alabama. They even built their program in the image of Nick Saban's.

When people tell me Alabama is lame, what I hear is they don't like defense. If you don't like seeing a team smothered by a good defense, then I understand. If a suffocating game plan isn't as cool as a high-flying offense, so be it. No matter the case, boredom or not, defense wins championships. If you don't believe it, go and look at the championship winning teams from the last 20 years. Look at their defensive statistics. Try to find a championship team like Baylor, or Oklahoma, who puts an emphasis on offense. Best of luck, my bored friends. You will find that task a tedious one.

The issue isn't boredom. The issue is that people don't like Alabama. Alabama has had tremendous games and moments throughout the last decade, and throughout history in general. I could name some off the top of my head. Does anyone remember when they played against Clemson in 2015-16? Both of those teams scored nearly 50 points. Alabama won the game in dramatic fashion. How about when Alabama beat Georgia in the 2012 SEC championship? That game wasn't boring in the least bit. Alabama won it in the last four minutes of the game after coming back from a deficit. What about when Alabama beat LSU in overtime? Does anyone recall Alabama beating Texas A&M and Auburn in shoot-outs? Shall I even mention the 2017-18 championship victory? That wasn't an exciting game?

It's very clear Alabama can win the shoot-outs, and they

also can win the defensive battles. They aren't boring. They are just good. They can adapt to any situation. Sometimes they lose and their flaws get exposed, but that doesn't mean they are boring. A true champion can lose and come back for their title. Alabama has done that time and time again. That's not lame. That's exhilarating to witness.

I'll tell you what's boring—consistent losing. I would rather watch Alabama win games 2-0 the entire season than root for a team that scores 60 points a game and loses because of bad defense. It's isn't cool at all to end the season without making a bowl game. Explosive offenses mixed with short-tempered defenses are lame. They sit on the couch and watch defensive teams play in titles games. I would rather pull weeds than watch a team like that play week after week. Okay, maybe not weeds, but I would rather wash dishes.

In the final analysis, this myth is ridiculous.

Myth Busted

Alabama has played in many games that were thrilling. They have won most of them. Winning isn't boring. A team with a great offense, bur shoddy defense, doesn't usually win a championship. If winning is boring, then what is losing?

Closing

I spent nearly seven years researching President Kennedy's assassination. Early on, I was fired up watching the conspiracy theories dance across my computer screen via Wikipedia. It was exciting to think there was a massive conspiracy involving a deep state. As time went on, however, disappointment settled in. I realized that despite all the plausible explanations of what happened to JFK, many originated behind falsehoods. What I'm saying is that once I worked hard at studying the claims people were making—many of them fell apart.

I could feel my mind grapple with what I wanted to be true and what the evidence said was true. I finally tapped out. I admitted most of the things I had read and heard were false, considering the facts. That's what I hope this book has done for you. There are mountains of myths when it comes to Alabama football. You will hear them repeatedly. They will sound logical. They might even convince you the program isn't what you thought it was.

The truth tells a different story. Alabama is legitimate in every fashion, and there isn't any credible evidence to say otherwise. I can feel people's minds exploding at that statement. They cannot fathom truths such as Alabama hasn't had an easy schedule for the duration of the current dynasty. They don't know how to tell their therapist that the referees didn't win those games for the Tide. They stumble to confess Nick Saban is actually likeable. And yet, they are now faced with a decision to make. They will either deny the truth or acknowledge it.

Now, because there are myth-busting facts available doesn't mean people will accept them. They most likely won't. If they did, they would have to admit Alabama is legitimate, and I don't see that happening. That's why this book is for you. It's for the Alabama nation. It's for the Riptide. It's not for the trolls who fly through the comment sections liking and commenting on everything anti-Alabama they can. They have accepted their lot in the college football world. They are okay with the Music City bowl, or the Crawfish bowl—I'm looking your way Ryan Anderson. They aren't *Tide Till They Die,* so they don't understand the Alabama way.

When you run into these people keep that in mind. Alabama represents to them something more than football as it does to us. Alabama is *the dark side* in their worldview. They are tired of seeing us win, as they are tired of seeing their teams lose. And yes, occasionally, when the stars align and the moon is full of red, Alabama will lose a game. I'm not denying we do. What I'm saying is the troll's teams lose more. That's why they cannot use statistics to defend their squad. All they have left is to hang on to the bedtime stories about Alabama football being a fraud.

This book is for you to know the truth: Alabama was dominate. Alabama is dominate. Alabama will continue to be dominate. It isn't a myth. It's a reality.

This morning I witnessed it firsthand. I saw a social media post where an Alabama fan was complaining that she's tired of defending Alabama's schedule. Well, fret not my Crimson sister! You can use the tools in this book to crush that argument once and for all. But, as a fan, I do relate to her struggle. I'm tired of seeing Alabama fans getting sucked into these black holes of sports talk.

Coach Saban once said the fans are a part of the program. He said we represent the Tide as much as he does. That's why he chews students out for not staying the entire game—by the way, if you don't want to stay, feel free to send those tickets my way! I think it's our duty as fans to defend the players' and coaches' work through the avenues available. We must flush the rat poison down the proverbial toilet. Our weapons aren't shoulder pads or helmets. Our weapons are facts infused with passion.

Do you want to do your part as a fan in fighting the myths that seek to destroy this dynasty? Then grab this book. Debunk the theories. Be proud of your team. Represent the Crimson and White.

I believe when we cast down myths, we help the program. This book is full of humor and joking jabs towards fellow sports fans. Yet, how much do these myths creep into a young recruit's mind after seeing them time and time again? How often has a sportscaster repeated them without fact-checking first? Will there come a day when Alabama misses a playoff opportunity because *they don't deserve it*. Public jurors are turning into public executioners in our culture. The louder they scream something, the more it seems true. We see this in all walks of life, not just football.

That's why this is important. When defend the program with facts, you assist in correcting the bigger picture. Will it change the trolls' minds? It probably won't. That's okay, because we aren't trying to change people's minds. We're just laying out the truth and letting it speak for itself. Deep down people understand Alabama is genuine, because they work so hard to find anything that might destroy their credibility. After nearly a decade it still hasn't worked.

One of the last points I hope to make with fans is that we want to have fun, but don't go overboard. Cursing someone out over a football game isn't going to make the program look better in the grand scheme of things. I'm not saying you should be pushed around, but try to do things with class. We don't want to be known as irrational or unreasonable. If someone makes a good point in a debate about the program, don't run from it or rationalize it. Admit that Alabama has flaws, but the program isn't an overall fake because of those flaws.

Alabama doesn't need us to get overly emotional in our communication. The team doesn't do that on the field, and the fans shouldn't do it off the field.

Do I sound unrealistic? Maybe I am. That's what Nick Saban wants from us though. He wants us to focus on the task at hand and eliminate the outside clutter. The outside clutter are the trolls who want to discredit the program, and the task at hand is destroying the myths they put forth to do it. So, show class in debating, but also have fun while you do it.

I hope you have enjoyed reading this book as much as I have writing it. I'm in a time of transition in my life and it's been therapeutic to work on this project. In a weird way it brings me back to an old comfort—Alabama football. It was the state I grew up in. It was the program I followed. It has brought me tremendous experiences as a person. That's why we're united together as fans.

I can't tell you how great it is to destroy these myths with you. Even though I don't know many of you, I do know the

Alabama culture. Throughout the last decade I've lived in Tennessee, Texas, Michigan, and Kentucky. No matter where I go, when I see an Alabama fan, we greet each other will a "Roll Tide!" Man, it doesn't get better than that.

That's why this book has been a joy to me. I want Alabama fans to have fun and know how great the program is. I want us to be able to appreciate the players and the work that's gone into every game we've won or lost. I want us to be proud to defend the program.

Most of all, I want Alabama to remain on top. I'll admit that. I'm a fan. How can I do my part? I do it through you. I do it when we all break the myths down together.

Roll Tide Roll!

Quotes

These quotes from Alabama football history can be utilized as tools in a debate. If you ever run out of ammunition while debunking the Alabama myths, you can grab one of these to reload.

"Mediocre people don't like high achievers and high achievers don't like mediocre people."

Nick Saban

"I'd like for people to remember me as a winner, because I ain't never been nothing but a winner."

Bear Bryant

"If you believe in yourself and have dedication and pride—and never quit, you'll be a winner. The price of victory is high, but so are the rewards."

Bear Bryant

"There's a lot of blood, sweat, and guts between dreams and success."

Bear Bryant

"The expectation level is high at the University of Alabama and it should be. What's wrong with people expecting excellence?"

Gene Stallings

"And believe me, to have been in the city of Tuscaloosa in October when you were young and full of Early Times and had a shining

Alabama girl by your side--to have had all that and then to have seen those red shirts pour onto the field, and, then, coming behind them, with that inexorable big cat walk of his, the man himself, The Bear--that was very good indeed."

Howell Raines

"In life, you'll have your back up against the wall many times. You might as well get used to it."

Bear Bryant

"The process is really what you have to do day in and day out to be successful. We try to define the standard that we want everybody to sort of work toward, adhere to, and do it on a consistent basis. And the things that I talked about before, being responsible for your own self-determination, having a positive attitude, having great work ethic, having discipline to be able to execute on a consistent basis, whatever it is you're trying to do, those are the things that we try to focus on, and we don't try to focus as much on the outcomes as we do on being all that you can be."

Nick Saban

"Talent is talent, and everybody knows somebody who has talent or ability, but they never really converted it into a productive performance for whatever reasons."

Nick Saban

"Discipline is not punishment. Discipline is changing someone's behavior."

Nick Saban

"I just love Tuscaloosa. I love being a part of The University of Alabama, and that is something that brings me a lot of happiness. The mindset across the entire University of Alabama is that we are champions, whether it is from an academic standpoint or an athletic standpoint. I love walking down the street in Tuscaloosa and somebody rolling down their windows when they drive by

and yelling 'Roll Tide.' There are just so many things about being a part of The University of Alabama and living in Tuscaloosa that bring us so much joy as athletes. Coming back for my senior year wasn't hard."

Damien Harris

"I don't think that too many people can deny the loyalty in the fan base of Alabama. It is one of the best, if not the best fan base in all of college football. There are people elsewhere in the country that can't even point out Tuscaloosa on the map, yet they're big time Alabama fans. I don't think there are a whole lot of schools in the country that are like that. You know, Alabama is just good like that."

Eryk Anders

"I think it's the work we put in the off-season. A lot of teams won't start working until after spring practice but we're hitting the weight room pretty hard soon after the season ends. Coach Cochran and the other guys do such a good job of training us. We're always searching for what we can do better. That's something Coach Saban does. He's the best coach in college football because he's willing to look at himself and change things, whether it be a routine for a bowl practice or even an offensive philosophy. He has his ways of doing things, but he's also willing to look at himself and ask if he can do it better and I think that keeps him ahead of the curve."

Ben Howell

"They set Alabama apart from all the programs. I guess every program believes that about their fans, but for Alabama, it's different. It definitely has the best fans in the country. It was crazy. To walk into class and have people congratulate you after wins was awesome. They rode the wave with us. They cherished the wins and they mourned over the losses. It just makes it what it is. There's nothing like it. We would sit at the hotel, and just

see thousands upon thousands upon thousands of people cheering, shaking the shakers at us, and just rooting our team on. You can just tell that a lot of these people live for those six or seven games a year at the stadium. They just take it to a whole new level. People talk about soccer Hooligan fans being passionate. The Alabama fans and the commitment and loyalty they have to that program is just mind-boggling."

Preston Dial

"I think Coach Bryant was misunderstood in a lot of ways. He was a great man. He was perceived to be a very hard and gruff type person, and he was very strong with discipline, but the thing that Coach Bryant did right was that he knew his players and he loved his players. He treated each of his players like you would a child. Some children you have to spank, and some children you just have to look at to get them to respond. Coach Bryant was a great people person. He knew how to motivate young men and he knew how to organize the staff. I think that probably his greatest strength was just dealing with people and getting the best of out his players. I know I was not a player of great ability, but I wanted to be my very best for Coach Bryant; all of us did. He knew how to get the best out of his players and to get them to play even better than they thought they could. I feel like that was probably his strength. He was a player's coach and he was a coach's coach as well. He had great staff and got the best out of those around him."

Keith Pugh

"Being a part of the University of Alabama football program has blessed me tremendously and helped me in more ways than one to develop into the person that I am today. I wouldn't trade my experience there for the world. There are lots of guys that you can talk to that played for other universities, and a lot of people have similar stories, but everything is just different in the Alabama locker room. I wouldn't trade it for the world. It was an amazing experience, some of the best years of my life. I got to know a lot of amazing guys and amazing coach."

Allen Skelton

"The process of repeating as National Champion requires more attention. It can't be about trying to prove something, because you've kind of already done that. It needs to be about: Do you want to be the best you can be? Are you driven to be the best player you can be? Are you driven to have the intensity, the sense of urgency, the intelligence? Are you going to work to do the things you need to do to be your absolute best? And that's not normal. Everybody thinks it's normal, but it's not normal."

Nick Saban

"The problem for Alabama is they are judged against perfection. Everyone else is judged against Alabama."

Paul Finebaum

"We just listen to Coach Saban and take in everything he has to say. Every game that I've ever been a part of that we lost he just said we have to come together and see what we did wrong. It's not about the other team. It's about us and what we did, and that's the biggest thing I take from Coach Saban. A lot of the guys come together and say we don't want to have that feeling anymore, so we push each other to go harder and be even better."

Jalston Fowler

"You see how he works day in and day out, every day. And then you see how exhausted you would be, or you are, at that time and he's still going hard, he's still attacking. It doesn't matter whether he was up all night or had to take a recruiting trip and come back. He doesn't have a tired side. He doesn't have a down side. And I'm the strength coach, so you think I can have one? No way!"

Scott Cochran

WRITE ME YOUR MEMORIES

It was a crisp November day when I watched Alabama defeat conference foe Mississippi State. I remember sitting in the seats with my dad, squinting my eyes through the sun in order to see the action unfolding on the field. It was just one of those days. Tyler Watts played well, and Alabama looked primed for a run at the SEC championship. That wouldn't happen though. Alabama was on probation at the time.

Yet, on that day it didn't really bother me. I was proud of the team and how they were playing despite the adversity in front of them. I wore my crimson shirt with pride. I could have sat in that stadium forever. If you're a fan of the Tide, and you've been to one of *those* games, you know what I'm talking about.

However, after many years of speculation, resolve, and conviction—it's finally time to confess to the University what I did after that game. To do that I'll need to explain how events unfolded that afternoon. I'll also need to explain my mentality as a 14-year-old, fanatical, Alabama fan.

On November 9th, 2002 I squeezed in between the fences leading onto the Alabama football practice field and stole a practice ball. It wasn't planned. Nothing was on paper or premeditated. It just happened. You see, during those days I ate, slept, and breathed Alabama football. As my dad and I walked back to the truck that afternoon I noticed how open the gate doors were. The chain link keeping it together was loose. We had decided to walk around the complex for a while to see the sights. It really was innocent—until it wasn't.

Once I saw the opportunity, I squeezed in between the gates and found myself on the other side. As my feet settled on the grass, I was mesmerized. Bear Bryant's famous tower was standing there. The field was beautiful with the sun settling upon it. I ran around freely. I recall being lost in the moment, and not having a care in the world.

As I ran up and down the field, I turned a corner and there was a group of footballs lying on the ground. In that moment I grabbed one to toss it around the field. I had no plans of taking it. I remember the smell of the leather. It had a worn out Nike emblem on it, and it stuck on your hands easily. In a moment, impulsively, I decided the University didn't need the ball anymore, and I took off for pay dirt.

My dad waited on the other side of the fence. He called for me to get in the truck. We were headed home. I suppose he was nervous with his son running wild on the Tide practice field. Little did he know, I was bringing a gift back with me. As I headed towards the fence, I remember thinking about getting on the other side as quickly as possible. That's why I made the decision. I tossed it over the fence, hearing it thump the ground and roll as I was squeezing in between the gate once more.

I imagine my dad was horrified at the time. Later, we would laugh at the thought of it all. He said he was waiting on me and saw a ball fly over the fence. As I frantically scrambled, grabbing it and heading to the truck, he wondered what to do. We left. He decided he would write the University a check for a donation.

Now that I'm older, I suppose that I wasn't displaying good character by taking the ball. I don't think Alabama would have let me have it. I don't think Coach Saban would be too happy with me about it.

It's just time, I guess. I need to apologize to the University. I'm sorry I took your ball. It just sat on shelves the rest of my years at home, and I honestly don't know where it is today.

If that ball could have made a difference in Franphony staying I wouldn't have taken it. Had I known the missing ball would have led to the coming years of turmoil I would have turned it back over to the University. I didn't though. I buried underneath my fanhood. I showed it off to friends. It became to me what Wilson was to Tom Hanks. Oh well, things worked out. Didn't they?

I hope the University can forgive me. I don't know if there's a statute of limitations on taking a practice ball, but I sure hope so. If I could, I'd throw it back over the fence, but it's deflated now. No, not because the Patriots got their hands on it. It's just due to time. Let me know how I can make it right Coach Saban and I'll do so.

In that moment, I represented all that is wrong with the world. I chose the pigskin over principle.

As goofy as that is, it's true. I don't condone it. I just wanted to share a memory of mine from my days as a fan. I also did this because I would love to hear some of your memories as fans. If you would like to write them down and email them to me, I will post them on my Facebook Authors page.

Please email them to me at:

jacobmarkuscarter@gmail.com.

A Letter to my Fellow Alabama Fans

As the years of winning continue, we have grown increasingly entitled. Empty seats, unreasonable demands, and ungratefulness for margin of victory have become a common thread within the Alabama culture. Once we lose a game, or go unchallenged for an extended period of time, we begin to nitpick the program. I'm guilty as well. It's human nature to want more, more, more.

However, the concern is driving Coach Saban into madness, or making the following seasons miserable due to dealing with complaining fans. We should be grateful for the times we are experiencing. We have had the privilege of witnessing a dynasty, and it's still ongoing. Do we want to spend the last few years micro-managing the team through critiques and inaccurate evaluations?

I hope not. I grew up during the Dubose/Shula era. I remember what it was like to lose to Auburn for half a decade. I remember not being able to compete in big games. I remember the yards given up and the anemic offensive performances. I don't mean to disrespect the players or coaches from that era, but it must be said for the sake of regaining perspective. We lost to Northern Illinois, Hawaii, and Louisiana Monroe. Let that sink in.

How easily we forget the desperation we had for a coach like Nick Saban in 2006. After years of probation and mediocrity, we knew change was on the way when Mal Moore hired him. He has exceeded expectations beyond our wildest imaginations. He's dominated the conference, tamed rivals, and reached the summit of college football five times. What else could we ask for?

I do understand the psychology of the Alabama fan. Sometimes the team becomes our identity. This can become unhealthy, but it's the truth behind our insanity. We can't stand losing because it somehow reflects us as a community. I get that. However, we need to remember what times were like before Coach Saban arrived and enjoy the fact that we are competing for a championship once again.

Alabama fans, please enjoy this year! Cheer your hearts out. Bleed Crimson. Support the players, coaches, and staff members at the University. Most of all: be thankful and enjoy the sport in its simplicity. Football, for all its issues, is meant as a gift from the Lord. We shouldn't worship it in place of Him, but we should enjoy it.

Roll Tide!

An Open Letter from Stan J. Griffin

Greetings to all Crimson Tide football supporters:

As you read this, Nick Saban's Alabama Crimson Tide squad is rolling toward yet another remarkable season, which was certainly expected. Ranked No. 2 in the preseason polls, most reasonable college football observers predicted the Crimson Tide to roll through the regular season, to once again battle for the Southeastern Conference title, and to also qualify for its sixth consecutive trip to the College Football Playoffs and its fifth straight appearance in the CFP championship game.

During the Saban era in Tuscaloosa, Alabama's presence at or near the top of the college football polls, and its place in the conference and national title games has become as much of a life certainty as death, taxes, and Donald Trump's shenanigans on Twitter. Let's face it, life is good enough for you anyway, being fans of the greatest program in college football history, with names like Bryant, Namath, Hannah, Jordan, Stabler, and Newsome among those illustrious names that have cemented Alabama's legendary status.

But during the Saban tenure at the Capstone, especially during the last 10 years, you have been richly spoiled beyond belief. During the past decade, utilizing constantly-changing coaching staffs and a multitude of talented players like Julio

Jones, Jonathan Allen, Mark Ingram, Derrick Henry, Amari Cooper and Donta' Hightower, Saban has led Alabama to five national titles and five SEC crowns. The Crimson Tide has been ranked No. 1 at some point in the season every year since 2008.

Every regular season game Alabama has played in since 2010 has had national title implications. And of course, I would be remiss if I did not mention the number of top-ranked recruiting classes Saban has collected since he arrived at UA and the staggering number of players he has sent to the National Football League. After a few rocky years that you had to endure with your beloved program during the coaching tenures of Mike DuBose, Dennis Franchione, and Mike Shula, the ridiculous level of success that Alabama has attained under Nick Saban has brought your swagger back.

And let's face it, Crimson Tide football fans are notoriously a little arrogant by nature. It just comes with the territory. Confidence, pride, and swagger are fine enough traits to possess regarding your excitement level about what Saban has meant to the Alabama program. And certainly, those traits are expected when you have been at or near the top like Alabama has under the direction of the Fairmont, WV native. But when your swagger and pride become increasingly interfused with doses of complacency and entitlement, it is not quite so desirable.

Unfortunately, there have been increasing signs of those unattractive qualities the last few years with lower attendance numbers from Tide fans at games, declining interest from UA students at UA home contests and ever-increasing expectations from Alabama followers. Almost unbelievably, there is even much more elevated criticism of Saban when Alabama, tragically, does not actually win the National Championship.

Expectations are fine, Crimson Tide fans, but not when you

begin to feel or even state that the SEC and National Championship trophies rightly belong in Tuscaloosa every season and that no other program is deserving. Sorry to tell you, but Dabo Swinney's Clemson Tigers refuted that notion in more than convincing fashion at the end of the 2018 season, and Alabama is going to have to work hard to prove it can be at that level of champion again, whether it is this season or future seasons.

Do not let your expectations and your complacency cloud or dilute your enjoyment of the amazing run that Alabama continues under Saban. Due to ever-increasing parity, and the lower number of scholarships available, this type of generational dynasty will never be seen again. All of us need to fully appreciate what Alabama has done and continues to do during Saban's phenomenal coaching reign in Tuscaloosa.

ROLL TIDE to all of you, and above all, take some time every now and again to simply savor and cherish what Saban's renown Process has meant for Alabama.

My Greatest Experiences as an Alabama Fan

I watched my first Iron Bowl on TV in 1999 when Shaun Alexander plowed through the Auburn defense. The next year, I went to my first Iron Bowl. It was raining and cold. Sleet lightly fell upon the stadium. Alabama had been ranked Number Three in the preseason that year. Andrew Zow and Freddie Milons were supposed to lead the team to the championship, but they ended up unranked at season's end. Coach DuBose was riddled in controversy. The shadows of a looming probation timeframe were lurking behind the locker room doors. Alabama lost to Auburn that day. It was a 9-0 game. It probably was the worst game I've seen content wise, but I didn't care as a young kid who was starting to bleed crimson.

I was enamored. The sights at Bryant Denny Stadium, mixed with the sounds of the crowd and million-dollar marching band, had me smitten. I was now a legitimate Alabama fan. The Crimson and White could do no wrong in my eyes, but that didn't last long. I soon found myself wearied by Alabama's underachieving. All I heard about growing up was the dynastic days of Bear Bryant. Where was that? Why did we struggle to even make a bowl game?

As any Alabama fan understands, the team becomes a part of who we are. It isn't so much that we *want* the team to win.

'BAMA FOOTBALL MYTHS

We *need* them to win. When they lose, we lose. When they taste victory, we taste it with them. When we talk about the program, we don't say "they." We say "we." It's an Alabama thing. Therefore, when the team was struggling to find their identity, I was too.

Throughout 2001, when Alabama was winning one week and losing the next, I felt the frustration of cheering on a struggling program. Even worse, Auburn seemed better than us that season, and soon we would travel to their house for the Iron Bowl. The season would end in shambles if we lost to them. Hope seemed to be dwindling. What happened next was one of the greatest college football experiences I've ever had.

Alabama upset Auburn 31-7.

I was elated. I had struggled and triumphed with the team all year. It was as if Andrew Zow had thrown those passes to me. I couldn't have been prouder.

The years went on. Alabama was on probation for recruiting violations. It decimated the program. Throughout the next five years we were mediocre, if not terrible. 6-7 and 4-9 records were endured by the fan base. Losses to teams like Northern Illinois and Hawaii made you sick to your stomach. It was depressing. I recall in 2005, however, Alabama had a pretty good team. They were strong defensively and wide receiving stud Tyrone Prothro was terrorizing opposing defenses.

On a crisp, sunny day, this Alabama team battled Florida and smashed them. The crowd was intense. Everything seemed to go right for us. We looked like a true contender for the first time in my life. Suddenly, Prothro broke his leg. Alabama ended up 10-2. Prothro never played again. Yet, I was again proud of the team because they overcame tremendous adversity.

After a couple more years of watching Joe Kines wrinkled

shirt walk up and down the sideline alongside Mike Shula, the time for change had arrived. Alabama fans were tired of being mediocre. The program seemed undisciplined and lacking direction. Rumors of Nick Saban being hired as the next head coach swirled. For an Alabama fan, this hire would be better than Christmas or any birthday party. We wanted him. In a way, the state needed him.

After Rich Rodriguez turned the job down all seemed hopeless. Would we ever get a legitimate head coach? Would we ever win a championship during my lifetime? Would Alabama even be a significant program after another decade of turmoil?

Then it happened. Nick Saban came to Tuscaloosa. For years, Auburn fans had gloated while beating our probation teams. I had endured the sickening times of going to high school after a loss and seeing the joy my Auburn friends carried. When Nick Saban was hired, that all shifted in one day. They knew it, and so did I. He gave his opening speech in front of the media, and you wanted to run through a wall. The days of dwindling in mediocrity were gone. It was time for teams to look at us and say, "I hate playing against those guys."

The first season Coach Saban was there was full of ups and downs. I went to the Tennessee game and watched Alabama destroy the Volunteers 41-17. It was the loudest Rammer Jammer I had ever heard in my life. If you don't believe me, go and watch it on YouTube. Alabama looked like they could compete for an SEC championship until their old habits came back to bite them. After a shocking loss to UL Monroe, and another loss to Auburn, fans were left frustrated. Yet, we knew what was coming. Coach Saban was recruiting some of the top players in the country. It was only a matter of time.

In 2008, Alabama destroyed a ranked Clemson team to start

the season. Our defense looked huge and quick. Our offense ran like a well-oiled machine. We had arrived and the entire college football world took notice. Alabama went on to go 12-0 in the regular season. I went to my second Iron Bowl, where we dismantled Auburn 36-0. The Rammer Jammer was played six times, once for each loss during Auburn's infamous streak. I basked in it with the rest of the crowd. It was an incredible moment to be a part of that victory.

The next year Alabama won the National Championship. While I had personal struggles in my life, this was a temporary relief. Alabama smashed Tim Tebow's Florida, winning the SEC championship. They went on to defeat Texas in the Rose Bowl and win their first National Championship since 1992. Watching the parade was surreal to me. Alabama fans lined the streets everywhere, chanting "Roll Tide" at the top of their lungs.

Where else can I go for that experience? I've been fortunate to be an Alabama fan during this modern dynastic run. Some of my other memories include watching Alabama defeat LSU and Notre Dame to win back to back titles. What about when Mark Ingram and Derrick Henry won the Heisman trophy? What about watching the 2014-15 team fight and claw their way into the playoffs? What about winning it all against Clemson, and watching Tua throw that bomb in overtime to do it again against Georgia? There were so many times they looked finished during those seasons. They always bounced back. Weekends became almost folklore to me. I did, in some way, relate the striving in my own life to their striving on Saturday's. All the little victories during the seasons meant a lot to me. I think they even had a micro-impact on my worldview. They wouldn't go away. They wouldn't give up. They always stayed in the game.

It wasn't just watching the team win that meant something to me. It was being a part of the team as a fan. I know a lot of times people want to claim fans are delusional for thinking they are just as important as the team, but I think they are. The team plays for the fans, and the fans cheer for the team. It's all a part of one cog at Alabama. It's a cultural mix. Ask any Alabama player who has played for the program if they understand how much they mean to the fans. They will all tell you something like this:

"They set Alabama apart from all the programs. I guess every program believes that about their fans, but for Alabama, it's different. It definitely has the best fans in the country. It was crazy. To walk into class and have people congratulate you after wins was awesome. They rode the wave with us. They cherished the wins and they mourned over the losses. It just makes it what it is. There's nothing like it. We would sit at the hotel, and just see thousands upon thousands upon thousands of people cheering, shaking the shakers at us, and just rooting our team on. You can just tell that a lot of these people live for those six or seven games a year at the stadium. They just take it to a whole new level. People talk about soccer Hooligan fans being passionate. The Alabama fans and the commitment and loyalty they have to that program is just mind-boggling. It's the history. It's kind of like being an American. You're proud of your heritage and you have your history. From Frank Thomas to Wallace Wade and Bear Bryant, all the coaches, including Gene Stallings, were amazing. They saw a lot of great teams. I think you combine that with their pride and they're extremely proud of the University of Alabama. They're also extremely proud of the state of Alabama. I think you combine that with a state that doesn't have any professional sports; they pour all of their heart and their soul into collegiate sports. In college, there's no other football team, as far as Alabama fans are concerned, then Alabama. It's not like Tennessee, where you can also be a Titans fan, or LSU, where you can be a Saints fan too. These folks are strictly Alabama Crimson Tide football fans; I think that's what really helps separate it."

Preston Dial

And that's what it's all about. I tie Alabama football into my childhood memories. It was a part of the good and bad. Just as they have had very difficult seasons, so have I. Just as they have had many exhilarating victories, so have I. They are like a familiar friend. I don't know how to explain it to you if you don't understand what it's like to grow up here. I've made many friends through being an Alabama fan. We've shared some incredible moments together watching the team achieve the heights they have.

It's not just a game to me. I don't watch because I'm obsessed with sports and can't focus on other things. That's never what it's been about. I watch because it's a part of who I am. It's a piece of the culture I grew up in. It's tied into so many moments from childhood to adulthood. That's why I bleed Crimson. Whether it was running on the practice field after the Mississippi State game as a teenager or going to Texas A&M to watch Derrick Henry run towards his Heisman, I've had personal experiences with the program that mean a lot to me.

I know you're the same. That's why I write these books. At some places they *play* football. At Alabama, we *live* it.

Roll Tide,
Jacob M. Carter

Thoughts on the Afterlife

I hope you find this old hymn, written by Edward Mote, as convicting and comforting as I have.

Jacob M. Carter

My hope is built on nothing less
Than Jesus' blood and righteousness
I dare not trust the sweetest frame
But wholly lean on Jesus' name
On Christ the solid Rock I stand
All other ground is sinking sand
All other ground is sinking sand

When darkness hides His lovely face
I rest on His unchanging grace
In every high and stormy gale
My anchor holds within the veil
On Christ the solid Rock I stand
All other ground is sinking sand
All other ground is sinking sand

His oath, His covenant, His blood
Support me in the whelming flood
When all around my soul gives way
He then is all my hope and stay

On Christ the solid Rock I stand
All other ground is sinking sand
All other ground is sinking sand

When He shall come with trumpet sound
Oh may I then in Him be found
Dressed in His righteousness alone
Faultless to stand before the throne
On Christ the solid Rock I stand
All other ground is sinking sand
All other ground is sinking sand

On Christ the solid Rock I stand
All other ground is sinking sand
All other ground is sinking sand

Author's Note

I have loved writing since I was a teenager. It's always been somewhat of an escape for me. I'm not a very creative person, but this is one area I enjoyed seeing flourish throughout my life. I've had many people help me along the way in that process, and that was crucial. I've had some successes and some failures, but I'm learning the key is to never quit. Really, that's the secret to writing for me—never quit. Keep improving. Find a topic you are passionate about. Research that topic thoroughly. Write about it until it hurts your brain to keep going.

The reason I say all of that is because I meet so many people who want to write a book, but they think they can't. You *can* do it. I promise you, you can do it. As for the notes in the book, please consider the following: I used quotes from my previous book about Alabama football called "The RipTide." It's an oral history that gives fans an inside look into coach Saban's program through the thoughts of his former players. All sources of quotes are given credit in the endnotes.

I was thrilled to have a forward and letter written by my friend, sports journalist Stan J. Griffin.

I ask you to please leave a review of the book on Amazon.com or your favorite social media outlet. It helps sell copies and spread the word.

If you have any questions, would like a signed copy, or would like to chat in general, you can reach me via at jacobmarkuscarter@gmail.com

Acknowledgments & References

Thank you to my publishers, Mike and Paula Parker. Thank you for all those who helped me with editing, proof reading, and giving much needed advice along the way. Thank you to my mother for her love. Thank you to all my friends and everyone who has helped me in my life with my walk with Christ. Thank you, Lord, for never letting me go. I love all of you.

1. Jacob Carter, https://bamahammer.com/2018/02/20/alabama-football-lucky-beat-texas-2009-championship/
2. Mike Gundy, interview with ESPN's Chris low, https://www.espn.com/college-football/story/_/id/27381802/i-am).
3. http://www.espn.com/college-football/playoffpicture/_/year/2009
4. Quote - Mark Inabinett, https://www.al.com/sports/2019/05/how-many-former-alabama-players-are-on-nfl-rosters.html
5. Quote - https://www.sportingnews.com/us/nfl/news/nick-saban-nfl-draft-alabama-players-coaching-career-dolphins/19rxhc7krvlwg1x94hvu96nypj
6. Quote - Christopher Walsh, https://bleacherreport.com/articles/2692417-the-biggest-myths-surrounding-the-alabama-football-program#slide1
7. Quote with Jalston Fowler, "The Riptide" by Jacob M. Carter, WordCrafts Press, 2016

8. Quote - Marc Tracy, Kirby Hocutt, https://www.nytimes.com/2017/12/03/sports/college-football-playoff.html
9. Quote - Chris Chavez, https://www.si.com/college-football/2018/01/02-how-many-national-championships-won-alabama-football
10. Quote - Joseph Goodman, https://www.al.com/alabamafootball/2018/12/dj-durkin-is-the-latest-coach-to-enter-the-nick-saban-coaching-car-wash.html
11. Quote - Brad Crawford, Joel Klatt, https://247sports.com/Article/Alabama-Crimson-Tide-Nick-Saban-make-Colin-Cowherd-Joel-Klatt-eat-words-125020065/
12. Quote - Doug Samuels, https://footballscoop.com/news/nick-saban-explains-how-discipline-works-at-alabama-discipline-is-not-necessarily-just-punishment/
13. Quote - Nate Scott, https://ftw.usatoday.com/2016/07/nick-saban-got-in-a-heated-on-air-argument-with-paul-finebaum-over-cam-robinson
14. Quote - Chip Patterson, https://www.cbssports.com/college-football/news/nick-saban-not-apologizing-for-bringing-jonathan-taylor-to-alabama/
15. Quote - Nick Saban, https://247sports.com/Coach/Nick-Saban-3/Quotes/
16. Quote - Jeff Fedotin https://nationalfootballpost.com/why-nick-saban-was-a-better-nfl-coach-than-you-think/

About the Author

Jacob M. Carter is a best-selling author, who currently resides in Kentucky. He's worked extensively on the topics of sports and history. He desires to see others also follow their passion in researching and writing.

Also Available From

WORDCRAFTS PRESS

Devotions from Everyday Sports
by Tammy Chandler

Never Run a Dead Kata
by Rodney Boyd

An Introspective Journey:
by Paula Sarver

Shameless Self Promotion
by Parker, Parker, & Martin

Elders at the Gate
by Ray Blunt

WordCrafts.net